Will the Real Jesus
Please Stand Up?

"*Will the Real Jesus Please Stand Up?* offers readers a clarifying and insightful comparison and contrast between the Jesus Seminar, on the one hand, and evangelical theologians, on the other. This book brings into sharp relief the contours of the debate and should serve well the Christian community—conservative and nonconservative alike."—Craig A. Evans, author of *Studying the Historical Jesus* and *Jesus in Context*

"*Will the Real Jesus Please Stand Up?* gathers together an unprecedented range of persons involved in the contemporary study of Jesus. Placing these key voices on the stage together, so to speak, gives us a feel for the texture of the discussion that belies typical us-and-them, black-and-white categories. The result for the reader is unparalleled access into how historical assumptions, faith commitments, and philosophical premises shape how we 'read' the historical Jesus."—Joel B. Green, co-editor of *Jesus of Nazareth: Lord and Christ*

"Genuine dialogue between evangelicals and members of the Jesus Seminar is very rare. This book is notable for the fairness of its format, and the forthright nature of the exchange, which is candid yet always civil in character. One could hardly find a better representative of the Jesus Seminar than John Dominic Crossan, and William Craig may be the best apologist for orthodox Christian faith at work today. The additional commentators and the final summaries of Craig and Crossan are extremely helpful. What the debate format may cost in clarity and precision is more than made up for by the liveliness of the exchange. An exciting, helpful book."—C. Stephen Evans, author of *The Historical Christ and the Jesus of Faith*

"The debate by William Lane Craig, a leading evangelical apologist, and John Dominic Crossan, a leader of the Jesus Seminar, found in *Will the Real Jesus Please Stand Up?* provides a helpful introduction to the issues involved in the modern discussion of the historical Jesus. The additional articles by four representative scholars responding to the debate help raise the key issue of whether 'the resurrection of Jesus' refers to something that happened to Jesus (Craig) or to his followers (Crossan)."—Robert Stein, author of *Jesus the Messiah*

"In *Will the Real Jesus Please Stand Up?* the reader is treated to a 'cutting edge' debate that takes us to the heart of what is being called the Third Quest for the Historical Jesus. We have the opportunity to look on while crucial aspects of the current debate are being discussed by several major participants, over a large range of topics. Thanks are also due to Baker Books for publishing noteworthy scholarly volumes when others have balked at the opportunity."—Gary Habermas, author of *The Resurrection of Jesus*

Will the Real Jesus Please Stand Up?

*A Debate between William Lane Craig
and John Dominic Crossan*

Moderated by
William F. Buckley Jr.

Edited by
Paul Copan

With Responses from
Robert J. Miller
Craig L. Blomberg
Marcus Borg
Ben Witherington III

Baker Books

A Division of Baker Book House Co
Grand Rapids, Michigan 49516

Published by Baker Books
a division of Baker Book House Company
P.O. Box 6287, Grand Rapids, MI 49516-6287

Printed in the United States of America

Library of Congress Cataloging-in-Publication Data

Craig, William Lane.
    Will the real Jesus please stand up? : a debate between William Lane Craig and John Dominic Crossan / moderated by William F. Buckley, Jr. ; edited by Paul Copan ; with responses from Robert J. Miller ... [et al.].
        p.   cm.
    Includes bibliographical references and index.
    ISBN 0-8010-2175-8 (paper)
    1. Jesus Christ—Historicity. I. Crossan, John Dominic. II. Buckley, William F. (William Frank), 1925– . III. Copan, Paul. IV. Title.
BT303.2.C73   1998
232.9′08—dc21   98-37884

Scripture quotations are taken from the New American Standard Bible (NASB), the New International Version (NIV), the Revised Standard Version (RSV), and the New Revised Standard Version (NRSV).

The book version of the debate between John Dominic Crossan and William Lane Craig is based on the audio version available from Pearl Publishing Company, P.O. Box 7, West Dundee, Illinois 60118.

For information about academic books, resources for Christian leaders, and all new releases available from Baker Book House, visit our web site:
                    http://www.bakerbooks.com

Contents

Acknowledgments

I am grateful for William Craig's extending to me the invitation to edit a book of such significance. It has been a privilege to work with Bill, a mentor and friend over the years, but I have also enjoyed collaborating with John Dominic Crossan, Robert Miller, Craig Blomberg, Ben Witherington III, and Marcus Borg, all of whom have been easy to work with and very encouraging. Jim Weaver at Baker Book House has been enthusiastic about this book from the start, and he has done much behind the scenes to get it off the ground. Ray Wiersma at Baker offered many fine suggestions to improve the text. Thanks go to Ron Turner, the initial sponsor of the debate, for giving rights to Baker to publish it. Special thanks go to my precious wife Jacqueline, not only for her wise recommendations, but also for her love and support throughout this endeavor.

Paul Copan
Oconomowoc, Wisconsin
August 1997

Introduction

Paul Copan

The Nicene Creed affirms:

> We believe in one God, the Father, the Almighty,
> Maker of heaven and earth, of all that is, seen and unseen.
> We believe in one Lord, Jesus Christ, the only Son of God,
> Eternally begotten of the Father, God from God, Light from Light,
> True God from true God, begotten, not made,
> Of one being with the Father.
> Through him all things were made. . . .
> By the power of the Holy Spirit he became incarnate
>   from the Virgin Mary,
> And was made man.
> For our sake he was crucified under Pontius Pilate;
> He suffered death and was buried.
> On the third day he rose again in accordance with the Scriptures;
> He ascended into heaven and is seated at the right hand of the Father.

How are we to understand this creed, which is itself an attempt to capture the heart of the Christian faith—"mere Christianity," as C. S. Lewis called it? Are the virgin birth and incarnation ("became incarnate from the Virgin Mary"), Jesus' crucifixion ("For our sake he was crucified"), and bodily resurrection ("On the third day he rose again") to be regarded as actual historical, space-time events? Or are they somehow mythological or metaphorical in that they express some more profound, superhistorical truths? Philosopher of religion John Hick, in his *Metaphor of God Incarnate*, recommends the latter approach—that we understand the idea of a divine incarnation as a metaphor. Only such a view makes sense in light of the new global consciousness, which ought to prompt in us a sensitive awareness of other faiths and cultures.[1] Thus we must speak of an

---

1. John Hick, *The Metaphor of God Incarnate* (Louisville: Westminster John Knox, 1993), 7–8.

incarnation only in the sense that Jesus, in his openness and responsiveness to God's will, incarnated divine love through his own selfless love.[2]

By contrast, Christians throughout the centuries have taken the virgin birth, incarnation, atonement, and resurrection to be real, historical events. The Nicene Creed has served as one of the church's standards for defining what a Christian must believe. To reject its statements, which are basic to Christianity, was to bring anathemas upon oneself, to be branded a heretic. Such was one of the consequences of removing faith from history. Indeed, if the doctrines of the creed are myths or metaphors, then the Christian faith, it has been believed through the ages, is undermined: "if Christ has not been raised, your faith is worthless; you are still in your sins," Paul writes in 1 Corinthians 15:17 (NASB).

Until relatively recently Christians believed that there is no radical disjunction between the Jesus of history and the Christ of faith. It was taken for granted that the latter depends upon the former. Yet over the past two hundred years or so, traditional Christians have had to contend with an alleged disjunction between the Jesus of history and the Christ of faith. Whether the Jesus of history and the Christ of faith should be closely linked sums up the thrust of this book, which takes the form of a discussion between theological conservatives and liberals—between evangelicals and participants in the Jesus Seminar—about the identity of the real Jesus. While I find myself at home within the former camp, I am convinced of the necessity of interaction between opposing or varying viewpoints. It often takes intellectual opponents to prompt us to think more clearly about our own position—and to prevent us from caricaturing or stereotyping.

The Christ of Faith and the Jesus of History

Before we get into specifics, it will be appropriate to give a brief historical background. Over the past two hundred years, three figures have significantly shaped the terms of the debate surrounding the distinction between the Jesus of history and the Christ of faith: David Friedrich Strauss, Martin Kähler, and Rudolf Bultmann. Strauss (1808–74) was the first to draw a clear disjunction between

2. Ibid., 105.

theology and history, between the Christ of faith and the Jesus of history.[3] In his *Das Leben Jesu, kritisch bearbeitet*, which was published in 1835 and later translated into English by the novelist George Eliot, Strauss attempted to undercut the supernaturalistic understanding of the Gospels. The traditional view of Jesus as the God-man and of the miracles in the Gospels belonged to the category of myth. These myths, while expressing important ideas, were not to be considered historical space-time events. If possible, they must be peeled away in order to properly piece together the historical Jesus. Strauss maintained that if we admit to the mythic viewpoint, then the "innumerable, and never otherwise to be harmonized, discrepancies and chronological contradictions of the gospel histories disappear" in one stroke.[4]

In Strauss's view the Gospels "present us with religious, not historical, truths."[5] While these religious truths may have some connections to history, they should not be regarded as formal history. By using the term *myth,* Strauss meant that the recorded events did not actually happen but represented the beliefs of the early church projected backwards.[6] That is, the origin of the theological truths about Christ is not to be found in history but in the early church's construction of myths about him. According to Strauss, "These narratives like all other legends were fashioned by degrees, by steps which can no longer be traced; gradually acquired consistency, and at length received a fixed form in our written Gospels."[7] During the time between the formation of the earliest Christian community and the writing of the Gospels there occurred "the transference of Messianic

3. Of course, Strauss's thinking did not take place in a vacuum. Enlightenment rationalism and G. W. F. Hegel's thesis of the gradual unfolding of history significantly influenced his thought. Earlier, Hermann Samuel Reimarus (d. 1768) had launched the quest for the historical Jesus, asserting that Jesus had attempted to establish an earthly messianic reign but died in disillusionment and God-forsakenness. Here we have the beginnings of a distinction between the Christ of the Gospels and the Jesus of history. With Strauss, however, this demarcation would become quite clear. See Craig A. Evans, "The Historical Jesus and Christian Faith: A Critical Assessment of a Scholarly Problem," *Christian Scholar's Review* 18 (1988): 48–49.

4. David F. Strauss, *The Life of Jesus, Critically Examined*, trans. Marian Evans (New York: Calvin Blanchard, 1855), 33.

5. Evans, "Historical Jesus," 40.

6. N. T. Wright, *Who Was Jesus?* (Grand Rapids: Eerdmans, 1992), 3.

7. Strauss, *Life of Jesus*, 35.

legends, almost all ready formed, to Jesus."[8] Thus very few of the myths in the Gospels were "formed entirely new."[9] They were the result of a "tide of religious enthusiasm" offsetting the "known religious dearth of that period [i.e., first-century Palestine]."[10] Strauss concluded that the cause of such enthusiasm need not be attributed to Gospel miracles.[11]

In Strauss, then, we see a vast chasm between faith and history.[12] Essentially, the Jesus of history and the Christ of faith do not even remotely resemble each other, as had been traditionally thought. In fact, Strauss considered his view that the Bible contains myths to be "directly opposed to the convictions of the believing christian."[13]

After Strauss, this bifurcating of history and faith was primarily carried forward by Martin Kähler (1835–1912). In 1896 Kähler wrote a short book entitled *The So-called Historical Jesus and the Historic, Biblical Christ,* which has had significant influence on twentieth-century Christology.[14] Kähler, alarmed by the subjectivism of some nineteenth-century theologians (Friedrich Schleiermacher, Albrecht Ritschl, and Wilhelm Hermann), sought to offer a more fruitful approach in order to preserve faith. He conceived of his task as twofold: "(1) to criticize and reject the wrong aspects of [the historical] approach to the life of Jesus and (2) to establish the validity of an alternative approach. The latter is the more important."[15] Kähler denounced the search for the Jesus of history with all of its critical historical methods as ill conceived, for it *"conceals from us the living Christ."*[16] Depending upon historical research to lay the foundation for our faith "will provide no real support."[17] For

8. Ibid., 69.
9. Ibid.
10. Ibid., 55.
11. Ibid.
12. Anthony C. Thiselton, "New Testament Interpretation in Historical Perspective," in *Hearing the New Testament,* ed. Joel B. Green (Grand Rapids: Eerdmans, 1995), 24. I am indebted to Thiselton's insights at various points in this introduction.
13. Strauss, *Life of Jesus,* 47.
14. See Alister E. McGrath's analysis of Kähler in *The Making of Modern German Christology: From the Enlightenment to Pannenberg* (New York: Basil Blackwell, 1986), 76–80.
15. Martin Kähler, *The So-called Historical Jesus and the Historic, Biblical Christ,* trans. Carl E. Braaten (Philadelphia: Fortress, 1964), 45.
16. Ibid., 43.
17. Ibid., 74.

Kähler, the historical Jesus was simply the fabrication of critical scholars. Instead, Kähler focused on the Christ of the Bible.[18]

Kähler assumed that "we have no sources for a biography of Jesus of Nazareth which measure up to the standards of contemporary historical science."[19] This is not to say that the Gospels are inadequate for purposes of faith. After all, the Gospels were written as testimonials or confessions from the perspective of faith: "the apostles already believed in Christ when they wrote about him; their witness was therefore already a form of dogmatics."[20] For Kähler, the real Christ is the preached Christ. The Christ of the Christian creeds is not at all the historical Jesus of critical scholarship.

Kähler's distinguishing (although not severing)[21] the Jesus of history from the Christ of faith enabled him to think of the Christian faith as based on the latter: the Christian faith is based not on who Christ was but on what he presently does for believers.[22] The historical method has little import for faith; it can do nothing to establish or negate faith. In a way, the intellectual attempt to recover the historical Jesus is a violation of justification by grace through faith. To engage in this endeavor is adding works to grace![23] Conversely, once one grasps by faith that God has through Christ extended his grace towards me (*pro me*), then—allegedly—Jesus need not be too firmly rooted in history.[24]

What exactly Kähler set out to accomplish is not obvious. What is clear, however, is that he significantly contributed to the dichotomy between the Christ of faith and the Jesus of history—a dichot-

---

18. Ibid., 76.

19. Ibid., 48.

20. Ibid., 44.

21. Kähler maintained that to proclaim Christ does not necessitate a distinction between "the memory of the days of his flesh and the confession of his eternal significance."

22. Ibid., 79.

23. Paul Tillich, who had been a student of Kähler's, writes in the foreword to *The So-called Historical Jesus*: "Kähler was a strictly systematic thinker who developed his ideas under the principle of the Reformers—'justification through faith by grace'—without repeating the traditional formulations of Protestant Orthodoxy" (p. ix). Tillich adds that Kähler sought to apply this Reformation principle to "the situation of modern man between faith and doubt" (p. x). Even those who doubt what Scripture or the creeds affirm can still be "accepted by God" and can "combine the certainty of acceptance with the actuality of even radical doubt" (p. x).

24. N. T. Wright, *The New Testament and the People of God* (Minneapolis: Fortress, 1992), 22.

omy that has shaped New Testament studies and systematic theology ever since.[25]

Kähler's focus on the preached Christ anticipated the work of Rudolf Bultmann (1884–1976). Like Kähler, Bultmann viewed the pursuit of the historical Jesus as an attack on Paul's doctrine of justification by faith. To seek in historical verification or historical probabilities security for one's faith is a failure of faith. Genuine faith does not need reinforcement from history. Hence Bultmann did not want to know Christ "according to the flesh" (2 Cor. 5:16 NASB). Instead, Bultmann asserted that all we can know about Jesus from history is *that* (*daß*) he existed. One cannot venture beyond this. Accordingly, the Gospels need to be "demythologized"; that is, the relevant kernel needs to be extracted from the outmoded husks of primitive supernaturalism, including miracles and exorcisms. Declaring that the cosmology of the New Testament is essentially mythical in character, and that the miracles of the Gospels are prescientific and primitive, Bultmann made his famous assertion: "It is impossible to use electric light and the wireless and to avail ourselves of modern medical and surgical discoveries, and at the same time to believe in the New Testament world of daemons and spirits. We may think we can manage it in our own lives, but to expect others to do so is to make the Christian faith unintelligible and unacceptable to the modern world."[26]

The gospel (or *kerygma*), Bultmann contended, is embedded in myth, which does not present "an objective picture of the world as it is."[27] Accordingly, we must not objectify God with language; we must not turn him into an object. Once we remove the husks—the myths—surrounding the divinized, miraculous Jesus, however, we come to the essential kernel of the Christian message: God has acted redemptively in Jesus, and we, realizing our desperate plight, are saved by responding in faith to the gift of God's grace. Bultmann also attempted to bring an existential component to faith: we personally confront Christ in the present when we respond to the

---

25. Markus Bockmuehl, *This Jesus: Martyr, Lord, Messiah* (Edinburgh: T. and T. Clark, 1994), 22.

26. Rudolf Bultmann, "New Testament and Mythology," in *Kerygma and Myth: A Theological Debate*, ed. Hans Werner Bartsch, trans. Reginald E. Fuller (New York: Macmillan, 1957), 5.

27. Ibid., 10.

preaching of the gospel; as a result, we enter into authentic human existence.

Only by demythologizing can Christian preaching be made acceptable to modern ears. The Christian message must eliminate any reference to spirits (whether malignant or benign), the historicity of New Testament miracles, and the doctrine of a blood atonement for sins. Nor can such eradication be selective: "The mythical view of the world must be accepted or rejected in its entirety."[28] There is no middle ground.

Consequently, historical research cannot help ground or buttress our faith. Rather, we must embrace the saving message of the gospel without reference to such research. Bultmann declared that "we have to discover whether the New Testament offers man an understanding of himself which will challenge him to a genuine existential decision."[29] Genuine saving faith, then, does not depend upon historical facts about Jesus of Nazareth.

Although Bultmann's and Kähler's motivations for separating faith from history were distinct from those of Strauss,[30] the result was the same: they all removed "theology and faith from the public domain of debatable inquiry."[31] Then in 1953 a significant turning point came when Ernst Käsemann delivered his lecture on "the problem of the historical Jesus."[32] He stated that without a solid connection between the Jesus of history and the Christ of faith, Christianity would collapse into docetism—a faith in a chimera. Since that time, the tide has turned in life-of-Jesus research: there has been a growing belief among New Testament scholars that the Gospels offer us useful and, in general, reliable historical information.[33] What we read in them about Jesus fits quite well with what we know about the setting of first-century Palestinian Judaism. As a result of the relinking of the Jesus of history and the Christ of faith, life-of-Jesus research

28. Ibid., 9.
29. Ibid., 16.
30. Strauss wanted to sift history from myth and thus destroy the Christian faith, whereas Kähler and Bultmann wanted to make room for authentic Christian faith by ridding it of historical concerns (Thiselton, "New Testament Interpretation," 26).
31. Ibid.
32. Ernst Käsemann, "The Problem of the Historical Jesus," in *Essays on New Testament Themes* (Naperville, Ill.: Alec R. Allenson, 1964), 15–47.
33. Here I follow Craig A. Evans, "Life-of-Jesus Research and the Eclipse of Mythology," *Theological Studies* 54 (1993): 3–36.

has shifted away from theological-philosophical presuppositions towards a more historical orientation.[34]

Enter the Jesus Seminar. The object of much media attention, it has implicitly revived the distinction between the Jesus of history and the Christ of faith. For instance, John Dominic Crossan, a former co-chair of the Jesus Seminar and a participant in this volume, declares in his *Jesus: A Revolutionary Biography* that the Gospels, when read comparatively, contradict each other; that is, they offer different interpretations of Jesus.[35] To resolve this situation, Crossan attempts, by utilizing proper "theory and method," to give an impartial picture of Jesus that is unclouded by credal interpretations of him.[36]

Other Jesus Seminar participants have argued that the historical Jesus must be rescued from the layers of theological encrustation added by his followers. What Christians have typically believed about Christ is far removed from the Jesus of history. Marcus Borg, another contributor to this volume, writes, "The notion that God's only Son came to this planet to offer his life as a sacrifice for the sins of the world, and that God could not forgive us without that having happened, and that we are saved by believing this story, is simply incredible."[37] In fact, to ask people to believe this presents an obstacle to embracing the Christian faith. The prominence afforded to such arguments has served to refocus attention on the dichotomy between history and faith.

The Debate

In October 1994, Dick Staub, a radio-show host in the Chicago area, invited Crossan to debate evangelical Christian philosopher and theologian William Lane Craig at Moody Memorial Church. Crossan and Craig discussed which approach was most appropriate for arriving at an accurate portrait of the historical Jesus. Syndicated columnist and author William F. Buckley Jr., whose sympathies clearly lie more with Craig than with Crossan (as is apparent in the debate), participated as the moderator.

34. Ibid., 15.
35. John Dominic Crossan, *Jesus: A Revolutionary Biography* (San Francisco: Harper, 1994), x.
36. Ibid., xi.
37. Marcus Borg, *Meeting Jesus Again for the First Time: The Historical Jesus and the Heart of Contemporary Faith* (San Francisco: Harper, 1994), 16.

The debate, which was sponsored by Turner-Welninski & Associates, was a lively interchange between conservative and liberal Christian perspectives on the identity of the real Jesus. The title of the debate and thus of this book, *Will the Real Jesus Please Stand Up?* was based on the popular television show *To Tell the Truth*. On this show three persons, each of whom claimed to be a certain individual, were questioned by a panel of celebrities. Then, on the basis of the responses, the panelists would vote for whichever of the three persons they thought was telling the truth. The climax came when the emcee would intone in a dramatic voice, "Will the real ——— please stand up?" And the real ——— would rise. This book asks a similar question about Jesus: Who is the real Jesus? Is the Jesus that Christians have been worshiping through the ages a legendary or mythological figure massively blown out of proportion by well-meaning followers? Or is he "the Christ, the Son of the living God"?

Two evangelicals and two participants in the Jesus Seminar were asked to respond to the debate and, in particular, to address the following questions:

1. To what extent can we distinguish between the Jesus of history and the Christ of faith? If this is a legitimate distinction, what lines of demarcation should be used to justify it?
2. Does the miraculous (i.e., divine supernatural intervention) have a legitimate role in explaining the historical data from the first Easter?
3. Whose reconstruction—Craig's or Crossan's—better fits the facts concerning the resurrection of Jesus? From the historian's point of view, where does the balance of probability lie?

In addition, all of the respondents raised significant questions about the proper approach or methodology for interpreting the Gospels.[38]

Speaking from his own Catholic background and his interactions with adherents of other religions, Robert Miller of the Jesus Seminar expresses his doubts about the validity of Christian apologetics, an endeavor in which Craig regularly engages. He offers the counter-

---

38. The two evangelicals were encouraged to read each other's response to the debate, as were the two members of the Jesus Seminar. The purpose was to minimize any overlap of content. Crossan and Craig did not read each other's final reflections before the book's publication.

example of Muslim apologetics, which adduces the uniqueness of the Qur'an, the radical message of Muhammad, and the remarkable growth of early Islam as vindications of its truth. In addition, he raises questions about inconsistencies in the Gospels' resurrection narratives and about the apocalyptic nature of passages such as Matthew 27:51–53, both of which call into question the historicity or literal nature of the Gospels.

Craig Blomberg's essay indirectly addresses some of the concerns that Miller raises, for example, the general reliability of the Gospels and the role of Christian apologetics. He also argues that although faith demands that we go beyond what historical evidence can show, it is not an absurd leap: "Historical evidence moves us a long way towards demonstrating our belief; as a result, the faith that is necessary to fill in the remaining gap is reasonable."

The third respondent, Marcus Borg of the Jesus Seminar, points out that while both Crossan and Craig affirm the resurrection, "each means something different." According to Borg, metaphors like the Easter story can be true irrespective of what happened to Jesus' corpse: "whether something happened to the corpse of Jesus is irrelevant to the truth of Easter." What is important is that Jesus' followers, whether in the first century or today, experience him as a living reality after his death.

The last respondent is another evangelical, Ben Witherington III. He devotes much attention to themes such as the importance of historical events for the very existence of Christianity, the materiality of Jesus' resurrection, and the theological significance of his resurrection. To reject the traditional understanding of Jesus' resurrection in favor of a metaphorical one is to embrace a view Witherington calls "Resurrection Lite."

After giving some background to his debate with Craig, Crossan offers a brief final reflection laying out the theological-historical presuppositions on either side of the debate.[39] He sees these presuppositions as the critical element of the debate and encourages further discussion between the conservative and liberal branches of Christianity.

---

39. It should be noted that Crossan declined the opportunity to expand his final reflection, which is considerably shorter than Craig's. He felt that the matter of theological-historical presuppositions was the most important aspect of the debate to address; he did not believe that discussion of the details of the debate would be fruitful.

Besides defending Christian apologetics, Craig's final reflection defends an implicit Christology on the basis of the consensus of contemporary scholarship. He points out that what he did in the debate was to take four well-established facts about Jesus and then make an inference to the best explanation—the bodily resurrection of Jesus, which is a divine imprimatur on Jesus' life and ministry.

It is hoped that the vigor and frankness of this debate and the responses will stimulate future interaction between the two groups. No doubt most of the readers of this volume will be in either the liberal or conservative camp. It is easy to become so entrenched within a particular viewpoint that we no longer take differing viewpoints seriously. In his treatise on the Holy Spirit, Basil the Great wrote: "Truth is always a quarry hard to hunt, and therefore we must look everywhere for its tracks."[40] Whatever side the readers find themselves on, it is my prayer that this book will help clarify their understanding as to who the real Jesus is—even if that means setting aside certain ideas and assumptions in order to search out the tracks of truth.

40. Basil *On the Spirit* 1.1.

Part **1**
The Debate

About the Participants

William F. Buckley Jr. is a syndicated columnist, the founder and editor of *National Review* magazine, and the host of the television talk-show *Firing Line*. He received his B.A. with honors in political science, economics, and history from Yale University. Buckley has authored *God and Man at Yale, Right Reason, Gratitude: Reflections on What We Owe to Our Country, In Search of Anti-Semitism,* and *Brothers No More.* He resides in New York City with his wife Patricia.

William Lane Craig earned a Ph.D. in philosophy from the University of Birmingham, England, and another doctorate in theology from the University of Munich, where, as a fellow of the Alexander von Humboldt Foundation, he extensively researched the historicity of Jesus' resurrection. Craig has been a visiting scholar at the Higher Institute of Philosophy at the University of Louvain and is currently a research professor at Talbot School of Theology. He has authored over a dozen books, including *Assessing the New Testament Evidence for the Historicity of the Resurrection of Jesus* and *Reasonable Faith.* He lives in Marietta, Georgia, with his wife Jan and their two children, Charity and John.

John Dominic Crossan is an original member and former cochair of the Jesus Seminar as well as chairman of the Historical Jesus Section of the Society of Biblical Literature. He earned a doctorate in divinity from Maynooth College, Ireland. His postdoctoral studies have been in biblical research at the Pontifical Biblical Institute, Rome, and in archeological research at the École Biblique, Jerusalem. Crossan has taught at several seminaries in the Chicago area and was professor of religious studies at DePaul University for twenty-six years. He has written over a dozen books on the historical Jesus—most recently such best-selling titles as *The Historical Jesus: The Life of a Mediterranean Jewish Peasant; Jesus: A Revolutionary Biography;* and *Who Killed Jesus? Exposing the Roots of Anti-Semitism in the Gospel Story of the Death of Jesus.* Crossan and his wife Sarah now reside in Florida.

1
Introduction to the Debate
William F. Buckley Jr.

My assignment tonight is to introduce the principles of this discussion and to moderate the debaters' exchanges. I will, as best I can, ask for elucidation when I think it necessary or interesting. What could be more interesting than the subject of the historicity of Jesus—that is to say, the factual knowledge of his life on earth?

The sponsors of the debate have circulated a few sentences from the late theologian George E. Ladd. They are, I think, worth contemplating:

> The uniqueness and the scandal of the Christian religion rests on the mediation of revelation through historical events. Christianity is not just a code for living or a philosophy of religion. It is rooted in real events of history. To some people this is scandalous because it means the truth of Christianity is inexplicably bound up with the truth of certain historical facts. And if those facts should be disproved, Christianity would be false. This, however, is what makes Christianity unique because, unlike other world religions, modern man has a means of actually verifying Christianity's truth by historical evidence.

First, we'll begin with eighteen minutes from Dr. Craig, followed by eighteen minutes from Dr. Crossan, who defends what one might designate the skeptical side. These opening addresses will be followed by rebuttals of nine minutes each. All of this will be followed by a forty-minute exchange, in which I will participate. And at the end of this evening's event will be five minutes for each of us in the way of a final statement.

If halfway through Dr. Crossan's speech he disappears in smoke, you will know that Jesus has cleared his throat!

24

2

Opening Addresses
William Lane Craig

As we near the end of the twentieth century, Jesus of Nazareth continues to exert his power of fascination over the minds of men and women. But who was Jesus really? Was he, as the Gospels portray him, God incarnate, or was he merely, in Professor Crossan's words, "a peasant Jewish cynic"?[1]

In tonight's debate I'm going to defend two main contentions:

I. The real Jesus rose from the dead in confirmation of his radical personal claims to divinity.

II. If Contention I is false—that is, if Jesus did not rise—then Christianity is a fairy tale which no rational person should believe.

Let's look then at the first major contention. Did the real Jesus rise from the dead in confirmation of his radical personal claims to divinity? First of all, in contrast to Dr. Crossan, the majority of New Testament critics today agree that the historical Jesus deliberately stood and spoke in the place of God himself. The German theologian Horst Georg Pöhlmann reports:

> Today there is virtually a consensus . . . that Jesus came on the scene with *an unheard-of authority*, namely, the authority of God, with *the claim of the authority to stand in God's place and speak to us and to bring us to salvation.* . . . With regard to Jesus, there are only two

1. John Dominic Crossan, *The Historical Jesus: The Life of a Mediterranean Jewish Peasant* (San Francisco: Harper, 1991), 421.

possible modes of behavior: either to believe that in him God encounters us, or to nail him to the cross as a blasphemer. There is no third way.[2]

Jesus' radical personal claims are blasphemous if they are not true. But the earliest followers of Jesus gave a good reason for thinking his claims to be true—namely, his resurrection from the dead. As the great systematic theologian Wolfhart Pannenberg explains:

> The resurrection of Jesus acquires such decisive meaning, not because someone or anyone has been raised from the dead, but because it is Jesus of Nazareth, whose execution was instigated . . . because he had blasphemed against God. . . . The resurrection can be understood only as the divine vindication of the man who . . . [was] rejected as a blasphemer.[3]

Thus the key to answering the question of who the real Jesus is lies in how we assess the resurrection of Jesus.

Let me share with you, then, four facts which are established by the consensus of scholarship today.[4] These provide adequate inductive grounds for inferring Jesus' resurrection.

Fact 1: After his crucifixion Jesus was buried by Joseph of Arimathea in his personal tomb. This fact is highly significant because it means that the location of Jesus' tomb was known. Now if his corpse lay in a known location, how could the belief in his resurrection have arisen and flourished? New Testament researchers have established this first fact on the basis of a variety of evidence:

 a. Jesus' burial is attested in the very old tradition quoted by Paul in his first letter to the Corinthians (1 Cor. 15:4).

2. Horst Georg Pöhlmann, *Abriss der Dogmatik*, 3d rev. ed. (Düsseldorf: Patmos, 1966), 230. To facilitate the audience's understanding, I translated Pöhlmann's Latin phrase *tertium non datur.*

3. Wolfhart Pannenberg, "Jesu Geschichte und unsere Geschichte," in *Glaube und Wirklichkeit* (Munich: Chr. Kaiser, 1975), 92–94.

4. Time permitted only an outline of the evidence during the debate. For detailed discussion and documentation see William Lane Craig, *Assessing the New Testament Evidence for the Historicity of the Resurrection of Jesus,* Studies in the Bible and Early Christianity 16 (Lewiston, N.Y.: Edwin Mellen, 1989). A popularization is available as *The Son Rises* (Chicago: Moody, 1981).

b. The burial story is part of very old source material used by Mark in writing his Gospel.

c. As a member of the Jewish court that condemned Jesus, Joseph of Arimathea is unlikely to be a Christian invention.

d. The burial story itself lacks any traces of legendary development.

e. No competing burial story exists.

For these and other reasons, the vast majority of New Testament critics concur that Jesus was buried by Joseph of Arimathea in his own tomb. According to the late John A. T. Robinson of Cambridge University, the burial of Jesus is one of the most certain facts about the historical Jesus.[5]

Fact 2: On the Sunday following the crucifixion, the tomb of Jesus was found empty by a group of his women followers. A number of reasons have led most scholars to this conclusion:

a. The empty-tomb story is part of the very old source material used by Mark.

b. The old tradition cited by Paul in 1 Corinthians 15:3–5 implies the empty tomb.

c. The story is simple and lacks signs of legendary embellishment.

d. The fact that women's testimony was considered worthless in first-century Palestine counts in favor of the historicity of the women's discovering the empty tomb.

e. The early Jewish allegation that the disciples had stolen Jesus' body presupposes that the body was in fact missing from the tomb.

I could go on, but I think that sufficient evidence has been cited to indicate why, in the words of Jacob Kremer, an Austrian specialist in the resurrection, "by far, most scholars hold firmly to the reliability of the biblical statements concerning the empty tomb."[6]

---

5. John A. T. Robinson, *The Human Face of God* (Philadelphia: Westminster, 1973), 131. Robinson, in refuting those who deny Jesus' entombment, states that Jesus' burial "is one of the earliest and best-attested facts about Jesus."

6. Jacob Kremer, *Die Osterevangelien—Geschichten um Geschichte* (Stuttgart: Katholisches Bibelwerk, 1977), 49–50. I have rendered Kremer's *Exegeten* as "scholars" rather than "exegetes" for clarity's sake.

Fact 3: On multiple occasions and under various circumstances different individuals and groups of people experienced appearances of Jesus alive from the dead. There are three reasons why this fact is almost universally acknowledged by New Testament scholars today:

a. The list of eyewitnesses to Jesus' postresurrection appearances which is quoted by Paul (1 Cor. 15:5–7) and vouchsafed by his personal acquaintance with the people involved guarantees that these appearances occurred. Included were appearances to Peter, the twelve disciples, the five hundred brethren, and James.
b. The Gospel traditions provide multiple, independent attestations of these appearances.
c. Researchers have noticed signs of historical credibility in specific appearances—for example, the unexpected activity of the disciples' fishing prior to Jesus' appearance by the Lake of Tiberias, and the otherwise inexplicable conversion of James, Jesus' younger brother.

The late Norman Perrin, a New Testament scholar at the University of Chicago, summed up the consensus of scholarship: "The more we study the tradition with regard to the appearances, the firmer the rock begins to appear upon which they are based."[7]

Finally, **Fact 4: The original disciples believed that Jesus was risen from the dead despite their having every reason not to.** Think of the situation the disciples faced following the crucifixion:

a. Their leader was dead. And Jews had no belief in a dying, much less a rising, Messiah.
b. According to Jewish law, Jesus' execution as a criminal showed him to be a heretic, a man literally under the curse of God.
c. Jewish beliefs about the afterlife precluded anyone's rising from the dead before the general resurrection at the end of the world.

Nevertheless, the original disciples believed in and were prepared to go to their deaths for the fact of Jesus' resurrection. C. F. D. Moule

7. Norman Perrin, *The Resurrection according to Matthew, Mark, and Luke* (Philadelphia: Fortress, 1977), 80.

of Cambridge University concludes that we have here a belief for which no prior historical influence can account; the only plausible explanation is Jesus' actual resurrection.[8]

Now Dr. Crossan realizes that once you agree to these four facts—namely, Jesus' burial by Joseph of Arimathea, the discovery of his empty tomb, his resurrection appearances, and the origin of the disciples' belief in the resurrection—then it's very difficult to deny that the resurrection of Jesus is the best explanation. So he finds himself driven to deny all four of these facts. Instead, he believes:

1. Jesus' corpse was thrown into the common graveyard reserved for criminals and was probably eaten by dogs.[9]
2. The women's visit to the empty tomb was a fabrication made up by Mark.[10]
3. The disciples never experienced any postmortem appearances of Jesus.[11]
4. The disciples never really believed in the literal resurrection of Jesus at all.[12]

Now at face value it seems quite implausible that on every one of these points the consensus of scholarship should be wrong and Dr. Crossan be right.[13] And that impression is confirmed when we ask, What evidence does he have for denying these four facts? What we discover is that Dr. Crossan has virtually no positive evidence for his claims. Rather, his conclusions are determined by his presupposi-

8. C. F. D. Moule and Don Cupitt, "The Resurrection: A Disagreement," *Theology* 75 (1972): 507–19; C. F. D. Moule, *The Phenomenon of the New Testament*, Studies in Biblical Theology, 2d series, no. 1 (Naperville, Ill.: Alec R. Allenson, 1967), 3, 13.

9. Crossan, *Historical Jesus*, 392–93; idem, *Jesus: A Revolutionary Biography* (San Francisco: Harper, 1994), ch. 6.

10. Crossan, *Historical Jesus*, 415–16; idem, *Who Killed Jesus?* (San Francisco: Harper, 1995), 181–85.

11. Crossan, *Historical Jesus*, ch. 15; idem, *Who Killed Jesus?* 202–8.

12. Crossan, *Historical Jesus*, xii, 404; idem, *Jesus*, 161–63; idem, "The Historical Jesus," *Christian Century*, 18 December 1991, 1203.

13. For a detailed critique of Crossan's alternatives, see William Lane Craig, "John Dominic Crossan on the Resurrection of Jesus," in *The Resurrection,* ed. Stephen T. Davis, Daniel Kendall, and Gerald O'Collins (Oxford: Oxford University Press, 1997), 249–71.

tions, presuppositions so bizarre, so implausible, that no confidence can be placed in the conclusions drawn from them.

Let me address just four of Dr. Crossan's presuppositions:

1. He thinks that the so-called Gospel of Peter, which is almost universally acknowledged to be a second-century forgery based on the four Gospels, actually contains the original account of Jesus' death and resurrection, and that the Gospel accounts are based on it.[14] No major New Testament scholar agrees with this view.

2. He believes that the Gospel of Mark is based on a prior Secret Gospel of Mark, which contained certain erotic elements which the biblical Mark found unsavory.[15] All but a handful of scholars agree that if such a document ever existed, it was a forgery based on the four Gospels.

3. He assumes that an early Christian community had so much "faith in the historical Jesus . . . that they were constantly inventing more of it all the time" on the basis of Old Testament stories.[16] British New Testament scholar Thomas Wright has called this "the most threadbare part" of Dr. Crossan's case since "the evidence points to precisely the opposite conclusion."[17]

4. Dr. Crossan has a serious problem: he's a naturalist. That is, he comes to the table already assuming that miracles are impossible. He states that "God does not act directly . . . physically, in the world."[18] In his book *Jesus* Dr. Crossan writes, "I do not think that anyone, anywhere, at any time brings dead people back to life."[19] Of Jesus' healing the leper he says, "I presume that Jesus, who did not and could not cure that disease or any

14. John Dominic Crossan, *The Cross That Spoke: The Origins of the Passion Narrative* (San Francisco: Harper and Row, 1988); idem, *Four Other Gospels* (Minneapolis: Winston, 1985), 131–74; idem, *Historical Jesus*, 375–94.

15. Crossan, *Four Other Gospels*, 162; idem, *Historical Jesus*, 415.

16. John Dominic Crossan, "The Historical Jesus in Earliest Christianity," in *Jesus and Faith*, ed. Robert Ludwig and Jeffrey Carlson (Maryknoll, N.Y.: Orbis, 1994), 20.

17. N. T. Wright, *Jesus and the Victory of God* (Minneapolis: Fortress, 1996), 63.

18. John Dominic Crossan, radio dialogue with Grant Osborne on *The Milt Rosenberg Show,* Chicago, WGN, March 1995. The full quotation is, "God does not act directly for me, physically, in the world in the sense in which the miracles taken literally would seem."

19. Crossan, *Jesus*, 95.

other one, healed the poor man . . . by refusing to accept the disease's ritual uncleanness."[20] And of Jesus' casting out demons he says, "I myself . . . do not believe that there are personal, supernatural spirits."[21] Note that these statements—"I do not think," "I presume," "I do not believe"—are just expressions of opinion. They are presuppositions with which Dr. Crossan begins. Well, if you begin your inquiry by presupposing naturalism, then of course you're going to come out with a naturalistic Jesus. The whole enterprise is question-begging.

Having been built on these false presuppositions, Dr. Crossan's picture of Jesus is simply not true. Thomas Wright says that Dr. Crossan's book *The Historical Jesus* is learned, inventive, and readable, but, unfortunately, it "is almost entirely wrong."[22] Similarly, the prominent Canadian scholar Ben Meyer praises the book for its readability and rapid pace, but concludes, "As historical-Jesus research, it is unsalvageable."[23] According to Howard Clark Kee of Boston University, its conclusions are "prejudicial" and "peripheral," not a "substantive development in responsible, scholarly study of the historical Jesus."[24]

In summary, there are good historical grounds for affirming that Jesus rose from the dead in confirmation of his radical personal claims. And Dr. Crossan's denial of this fact is based on idiosyncratic presuppositions which no other serious New Testament critic accepts.

That brings us to our second contention: If Jesus did not rise in confirmation of his claims, Christianity is a fairy tale which no rational person should believe. This point seems fairly obvious. As the apostle Paul wrote, "If Christ has not been raised, your faith is futile and you are still in your sins" (1 Cor. 15:17 RSV). If Jesus wasn't who

20. Ibid., 82. He goes on to say, "Miracles are not changes in the physical world so much as changes in the social world."

21. Ibid., 85.

22. Wright, *Victory of God*, 44.

23. Ben F. Meyer, review of *The Historical Jesus*, by John Dominic Crossan, *Catholic Biblical Quarterly* 55 (1993): 576. According to Meyer, "the judgments that have allowed [Crossan] to broaden and reshape the data base (by positing surprisingly early dates for several apocryphal works) are eccentric and implausible" (p. 575).

24. Howard Clark Kee, "A Century of Quests for the Culturally Compatible Jesus," *Theology Today* 52 (1995): 28. Kee also complains that Crossan's conclusions "are inherent in the presuppositions and methods" he has chosen to adopt from the outset (p. 17).

the Gospels say he was, then believing in him would be just as silly as believing in Santa Claus or the Easter Bunny. We might believe in what these mythical figures represent, say, the spirit of giving in the case of Santa Claus; but we wouldn't believe in Santa Claus himself. Similarly, if Jesus was just a social revolutionary, then we might believe in some of the things he stood for, say, universal human rights; but we wouldn't believe in him. In particular, we wouldn't worship him; we wouldn't pray to him or entrust our lives to him or think he loves us. If we did, we would either be worshiping and praying to a dead man, which is literally idolatry, or else be worshiping and praying to a figment of our imagination, which is self-delusion.

Now, as I say, this seems to me to be just common sense. Yet, incredibly, Dr. Crossan thinks that we should keep on worshiping Christ and going to church and so forth, even though the historical Jesus wasn't at all what the church says he was. Dr. Crossan says that regardless of what the historical facts are, Christians affirm by faith that Jesus is divine; and so for them he *is* divine.[25] If they just believe hard enough, it somehow becomes true.

Now Dr. Crossan's views on this matter are not original. Another famous person said much that same thing. He said that all we need is trust and faith—and a pinch of pixie dust. Then, if we think of the happiest things, it will be as if we have wings. We will be able to fly, off to Never Land. May I submit to you that Peter Pan theology, however charming and erudite, is irrational? Any interpretation of reality not in accord with the facts about reality is just a fairy tale which no rational person should believe. It is not a rational thing to do—to worship and pray to somebody who isn't really there, or to think that he is there, no matter what the facts, just because one believes in him.

Fortunately, we have no need to engage in such theological salvage operations. The essential historical facts undergirding Jesus' resurrection are acknowledged by the majority of biblical critics. The Christ of faith, who lives in my heart today, is the same person who once walked the shores of Galilee, hung on a Roman cross, and rose triumphantly from the tomb for our salvation.

---

25. Crossan, *Who Killed Jesus?* 215–16. Crossan's views on the relationship of history and theology are a strange and inconsistent blend of nineteenth-century liberalism, Bultmannian existentialism, and contemporary postmodernism.

John Dominic Crossan

In my opening statement I'll try to explain to you the presuppositions from which I work, at least as clearly as I can see them. I'll have two major points—one concerning history and one concerning language. And then I'll say why I consider those points to be important.

The first point has to do with history. By way of introduction I emphasize the difference between the real Jesus and the historical Jesus. The title of this debate refers to "the real Jesus," who is the Jesus of two thousand years of Christian faith. Who he is is very easily answered, but I have never used the phrase "the real Jesus" in any book. Possibly that may be because I learned English in Ireland rather than America, and I don't use "real" quite so often as it is used here. It will be on the front page of tomorrow's *New York Times* "Book Review" section—"The Real Lives of the Brontës." In such a sense I use instead "the historical Jesus" because that is the technical term in scholarship. Whether we like it or not, it's a technical term.

The Society of Biblical Literature, to which Dr. Craig and I belong, has a section called the Historical Jesus Section, which attempts to talk about the earthly Jesus as he can be reconstructed through historical means. So that's what I've usually been talking about. The real Jesus is, of course, much bigger than the historical Jesus.

In reconstructing the historical Jesus, a few historical presuppositions are important for me. And by "presupposition" I do not mean at all something that cannot be challenged. It simply means something that I started from. If it's wrong, then I have to start all over again.

The presuppositions with which I begin are supported by a massive consensus of scholarship. That's not an argument; that's just a statement of fact. I do not find any passage in the New Testament (or anywhere in the Bible, in fact) that tells us that numbers make us right, that the majority is usually moral. As a matter of fact, there seems to be a tendency in the Bible to think that the few are more likely to be right than the many.

Here is one presupposition: the Gospel of Mark was used by the Gospels of Matthew and Luke. It was one of their major sources. That is where I begin. If that is wrong, everything will have to be re-done. And, of course, it could be proved wrong. It could be proved wrong by a peasant's digging around in Egypt tomorrow morning in a rubbish dump and finding, say, a Gospel dated to the year 100. But if Mark was used by Matthew and Luke, then you can (by putting them in parallel columns, which is the way scholars study them) see what Matthew and Luke have done with Mark. You can see, in other words, how inspiration operates when somebody is using a source. That will become crucial as we continue.

A second presupposition for which there is also a massive consensus of scholarship (I am stating that simply as a fact) is that in the data of the New Testament Gospels covering Jesus' words and deeds, there are three successive layers. Let's call the first one, which goes back to Jesus, the original layer; the second layer is the tradition that took and creatively adapted the sayings and works of Jesus; the third layer comes from the Evangelists themselves. Now there is a degree of creativity in all of those layers that somewhat bothers us.

Without those presuppositions everything that I say would be as absurd as Dr. Craig has made it sound. With those presuppositions, we start down a long two-hundred-year voyage. And the challenge is not to lose your nerve.

Gospels are exactly what they say they are—"good news"— which means they must be good and they must be news. They're good from somebody's point of view—the Christian point of view, not the pagan Roman point of view. And they are news. That means, by definition, that Gospels update. Mark updates to the seventies. Matthew and Luke update, say, to the eighties. John updates to the nineties. Note that I say "update," not "upgrade." They update the story. Those, then, are my presuppositions (not beyond discussion, of course), and if they are wrong, everything built on them is built on sand.

As soon as we say that Matthew and Luke are based on Mark, and as soon as we say (going a little bit further) that John possibly knew the works of Matthew, Mark, and Luke, we begin to see not four accounts about Jesus, but a stream of developing tradition. By

34

the way, I see no problem with that. I think if we had the Evangelists here, they would say that is called the freedom of the children of God. That's what it means to have the Holy Spirit: "I, Matthew, am willing to look at Mark's telling me what Jesus said and respond for my people. Right now, this is a better way to say it. I too have the Holy Spirit, Mark."

In the last two hundred years, the formulation of the question we are discussing has, unfortunately, been the historical Jesus over against the Christ of faith. That is a formulation which I reject completely. It is not "over against"; it is, rather, a question of the relationship.

The way I formulate the question is this: If we were neutral observers in Palestine in the first quarter of the first century, what would we have seen? What would explain to us why some people said, "This man is divine. Let's follow him," and why other people—maybe equally good people—said, "This man is criminal. Let's execute him"? We know for a fact that both groups were there. How would we explain the two—not just the Christian point of view, but the pagan point of view as well? I am totally on the Christian side, but I have to ask myself, "What were the pagans seeing that they found criminal?"

A second major point, which is really much more important for me than the former, has to do with language and with the distinction between literal and metaphorical language (or actual and symbolic language, if you prefer). Most of us understand completely that the sentence "Jesus lived at Nazareth" is actual, factual, historical, biographical—whatever you would call it. The sentence "Jesus is the Lamb of God" we know immediately is not the same type of language. It is symbolical, and we have to ask what it means. It is figurative; it is metaphorical. Now stories are like that—some stories are literal and others are symbolical, and, of course, either can be true or false.

Let me take you out of the Bible. Since Dr. Craig went to Peter Pan, I can go into Never Never Land too. Let's go to Aesop—Aesop's fables—and imagine a three-way argument. One person says, "Did you know animals could talk in ancient Greece?"

A second person says, "No, no, no. They couldn't, but there was a stupid Greek who thought they could."

And, of course, the third person says, "Wait a minute. You're both wrong. Aesop told a certain type of story—a genre called fable. Animals are allowed to talk there to make basic moral principles evident."

Now how could I today prove that animals could or couldn't speak in ancient Greece? I'd hate to have Johnnie Cochran coming after me in court on that one:

"Were you there, Dr. Crossan?"

"No, I wasn't."

"Have you checked out *all* the animals?"

"Well, no, I haven't."

"Then how dare you say what could or could not happen in ancient Greece!"

"Well, animals don't usually talk."

"That's a prejudice, Dr. Crossan; that's a presupposition."

"Well, yeah, I guess."

But what we have just done is to miss the whole point of Aesop's fables. Each of his stories had a moral point, and we're missing it. We're now arguing whether animals could or could not talk in ancient Greece, and whether the ancient Greeks were stupid enough to think they could. This argument is totally misguided.

Now let's move from fable to parable. Jesus tells the story of the good Samaritan (and notice by the way that Jesus likes parables). Imagine, if you will, a similar argument:

"Did the good Samaritan parable really happen?"

"Of course it did. It mentions Jerusalem. It mentions Jericho. It mentions going down that 1,500-foot drop. It mentions the bandits, and everyone knows there were bandits in the hills around there. Of course it's historical."

"No, it isn't historical. Jesus just made it up. It's a parable, dummy!"

Now watch what's happening. There's an argument going on which cannot be proved one way or the other. We could make a very good case that Jesus' parable was historical. We could also make a very good case that Jesus made it up on the spot. In the meanwhile we are avoiding the issue, which is Jesus' challenge to live life like the good Samaritan, to live life not in ethnic cleansing, but in doing everything possible to help others in distress, even an enemy. Are we willing to live life like that? That's the question. About whether the story is historical or not, I'd almost say, "I don't care." The debate over historicity may be interesting, but it must not be allowed to fake us out on the real issue.

Let me go into the Bible. I'm going to talk about two examples of beginnings, and I'll speak of figurative, symbolical, parabolic language (I won't use the term "mythical language" because I'm afraid it sounds like a dirty word at the moment). Parable is a form of language Jesus chose, a form he may have picked up from his Father. There's a lot of parabolic language in the Bible. Parabolic language is regularly found at biblical beginnings and endings, because beginnings have to carry our hopes, and endings have to bury our fears. So endings and beginnings are freighted heavily with symbolic language.

I open my Bible to Genesis 1, and I find that God created the world in six days of labor (or six days of command) and one day of rest. I immediately ask myself, "Is this information about the beginning of the world? It certainly reads that way." But two factors come together to push me not to read it that way. One comes from reason, and the other comes from revelation. And reason and revelation are, for me, gifts from God. (As an aside, I reject absolutely the naturalist position that Dr. Craig attributed to me.) Reason comes from God to all of us; revelation comes from God to some of us. Reason tells us about evolution, and it sounds reasonable that instant six-day creation is not the way in which the world came to be. That could all be wrong, of course. But it sounds reasonable that evolution is how it happened.

I ask a more important question—and this is really the crucial question for me: Is the biblical story of creation trying to tell us something else? Is it a metaphorical story that we read literally before the Enlightenment and consequently got it all wrong? And if it is a metaphorical story, what's the metaphorical story about? Well, read it again. God cannot skip the Sabbath even to create the world. He can't begin on Wednesday, for example, and work straight through till Tuesday. God has to observe the Sabbath. The Sabbath is bigger than creation; it's very close to being bigger than God. The challenge of the creation story to me is, then, Do I or do I not believe that God is Lord of time, Lord of history, and—when I find out about it—Lord of evolution?

We could of course argue—and not be able to prove it one way or the other—that "six days" means six days; "morning and evening, one day" or "evening and morning, one day" (in the Jewish reckon-

37

ing) means just what it says. In the meanwhile, however, we would be avoiding the major issue that the story gives us as its challenge: Is God the Lord of history? And if so, what are we doing about it?

Let me come then to another beginning—the beginning of Jesus' life. Note again how figurative language weighs heavily in beginnings and endings. I read Luke and Matthew, and very, very clearly (as clearly as those six days) I read that there was a virginal conception, a miraculous conception, in which God overshadowed Mary. God and Mary produced Jesus; therefore, Jesus is divine, Jesus is the Son of God. Now immediately my reason says, "Wait a minute. Do such things really happen?"

I hear the murmurs: How can I tell? I wasn't there. Maybe this is the exception, but then I know there's a similar story. This other ancient story is found in Suetonius, the Roman historian, who tells us that the night Augustus (the emperor at the time of Jesus' birth) was conceived, his mother Atia was in the temple of Apollo, and Apollo impregnated her so that Atia bore a divine child. "Augustus is the Son of God and divine," says the pagan Roman. "Jesus is Son of God and divine," the Christian believes.

As I look at those two stories, I'm sure we could give reasons not to disbelieve Suetonius: he's not a liar, and so on. What about those two stories? Here is how I read them. One could say that the story of Jesus is historical, but the pagan Roman story is mythical. Since there are no pagan Romans around to defend it, and it's not politically incorrect to knock the pagan Romans, one would probably get away with classifying the two stories differently. But in all honesty the question then presses: Did Matthew and Luke intend their accounts literally, or did they intend them metaphorically? Are we misreading them? Are we misinterpreting them? And are our debates about the biology of Mary totally off the point?

The point is this: Where do we find our God? Do we find our God in Augustus in a Palatine palace backed by legions with power from the top down? Or do we find our God in a child born in a peasant stable to a family that didn't even have a place for the mother to deliver? Where do we find our God? With power? With domination? With Augustus? Or with Jesus and empowerment from the bottom up? That's the challenge, and that's what we're avoiding by asking historical questions.

When Christians said in the first century, "Jesus is Lord," they were committing high treason. They meant, "Jesus is Lord, and Caesar ain't." It took the Romans about a hundred years to figure out that the Christians were serious on that score, and it wasn't just some kind of a bad joke. By then it was too late. It was as if in the 1930s a group in Germany began to say, "Jesus is Führer," meaning Hitler ain't.

That is the challenge of the biblical stories. The question is, "Did people in ancient times and in medieval times and do people in many places of the world today know how to hear a story—even if they are not really sure whether it is literal or metaphorical—and get the point?" And then comes the question, "Do we or do we not believe in that point? Is Jesus Lord and Savior for us or not? And if Jesus is, Caesar is not. (But we're Caesar now.)"

Why is this important for me? For two reasons—internal and external. The Gospels are normative, I think, for us as Christians not just in their production, in what they have created, but in the way they are written. A Gospel goes back, as it were, to the twenties. It writes Jesus from the twenties into the seventies, the eighties, the nineties. A Gospel always takes the historical Jesus and laminates him together with the Christ we believe in—the two of them together. John rewrites the twenties as Mark had done before him. The historical Jesus remains crucial for Christianity because we must in each generation of the church redo our historical work and redo our theological work. We can't skip it.

The second reason is this. When I look a Buddhist friend in the face, I cannot say with integrity: "Our story about Jesus' virginal birth is true and factual. Your story that when the Buddha came out of his mother's womb, he was walking, talking, teaching, and preaching (which I must admit is even better than our story)—that's a myth. We have the truth; you have a lie." I don't think that can be said any longer, for our insistence that our faith is fact and that others' faith is a lie is, I think, a cancer that eats at the heart of Christianity.

3

William Lane Craig's Rebuttal

In this speech I'd like to review those two contentions that I said I would defend tonight and see how Dr. Crossan's replies measure up. First, you remember I argued that the real Jesus rose from the dead in confirmation of his radical personal claims to divinity. I pointed out that Jesus made radical claims to divine authority by which he put himself in the place of God, and Dr. Crossan didn't deny that. I then said that Jesus' resurrection from the dead stands as confirmation of those claims, and I pointed out four facts that are agreed upon by scholarship today: the burial by Joseph of Arimathea, the empty tomb, the resurrection appearances, and the origin of the disciples' belief in the resurrection. These are established historical facts, and the best explanation for them, I believe, is the resurrection of Jesus.

Dr. Crossan denies these four established facts on the basis of several radical presuppositions which I think are simply false and which therefore present to us an untenable picture of Jesus. In his speech Dr. Crossan said, "Well, I have two other presuppositions—first, that Mark was used by Matthew and Luke; and, second, that there are three layers of tradition." I certainly accept both of those presuppositions. What I do not accept, however, is that the Gospel accounts of the death and resurrection of Christ are based on the Gospel of Peter, that Mark is based on a Secret Gospel of Mark, that there was this inventive early Christian community, and that naturalism holds. Those are the controversial presuppositions, not Markan priority or three layers of tradition. Dr. Crossan said that he rejects naturalism, but I quoted his statement that "God does not act directly . . . physically, in the world," as well as several other examples. Now if he wants to back away from that naturalistic view, that's fine. (Naturalism is the view that there are no miracles in the world, and that's what he asserts in his writings.) I don't think we've seen anything that directly refutes my first (and I think, major) contention tonight.

Now what about the second point? If Jesus did not rise, then Christianity is a fairy tale which no rational person should believe. Here I presented a dilemma. If the historical Jesus is not identical to the Christ of faith, then to continue to worship and pray to the Christ of faith is either idolatry (worshiping and praying to a dead man) or self-delusion (worshiping and praying to a figment of one's imagination). Now what Dr. Crossan said here is that the real Jesus is not the same as the historical Jesus. Why? Well, because we use metaphorical and literal language to express different truths. He points out that Aesop's fables and the parables of Jesus are not used to express literal truths; rather, they are metaphorical.

That's certainly true as a general point. But the question is, What is the literary genre that we're dealing with? What type of literature are the Gospels? Now Dr. Crossan knows that the Gospels are not of the genre of myth or allegory or folk story or fairy tale. They're of the genre of historical writing. This has been excellently demonstrated by Colin Hemer in his recent volume *The Book of Acts in the Setting of Hellenistic History*.[1] Combing through the Book of Acts, Hemer finds a wealth of historical detail that has been verified by archeological and papyrological findings. These findings show that Luke is a consummate historian in the Book of Acts (and I believe also in the Gospel of Luke). The judgment of Sir William Ramsay still stands: "Luke is a historian of the first rank . . . this author deserves to be placed among the very greatest of historians."[2]

Now what about the specific examples Dr. Crossan gives? What about the virgin birth? He compares this to pagan birth stories. Well, I would simply suggest that the virgin birth story in Matthew and Luke is not parallel to stories in pagan literature. In fact, it is unparalleled by anything in pagan literature. Ben Witherington summarizes well:

> Any comparison of Matthew 1–2 and Luke 1–2 to pagan divine birth stories leads to the conclusion that the Gospel stories cannot be explained simply on the basis of such comparisons. . . . For what we find in Matthew and Luke is not the story of . . . a divine being descending to earth and, in the guise of a man, mating with a human woman, but

1. Colin J. Hemer, *The Book of Acts in the Setting of Hellenistic History*, ed. Conrad H. Gempf (Tübingen: J. C. B. Mohr, 1989).
2. William Ramsay, *The Bearing of Recent Discovery on the Trustworthiness of the New Testament* (London: Hodder and Stoughton, 1915), 222.

rather the story of miraculous conception without the aid of any man, divine or otherwise. As such, this story is without precedent either in Jewish or pagan literature.[3]

So I don't think the virgin birth story can be written off as being on the level of pagan mythology.

But what specifically about the resurrection? When the New Testament writers speak of the resurrection, are they speaking metaphorically? Well, I think this is very clearly not their intention; they intend the resurrection to be taken as a literal event. Raymond Brown, a great contemporary New Testament scholar, writes, "It is not really accurate to claim that the NT references to the resurrection of Jesus are ambiguous as to whether they mean bodily resurrection—there was no other kind of resurrection."[4] The Jews believed in a bodily, physical resurrection from the grave. And thus you find, for example, the apostle Paul in 1 Corinthians 15 discoursing at length in answer to the question "How are the dead raised? With what kind of body do they come?" (v. 35 RSV). The sermons in the Book of Acts similarly present the resurrection as a literal event in history, just like the crucifixion and the burial of Jesus—events verified by witnesses. And the whole empty-tomb tradition shows that the resurrection was not thought of as a mere metaphor but as a literal event.

Dr. Crossan's view is that the resurrection is just a metaphor for the "continuing presence of Jesus."[5] But the early Christians could have expressed the continuing presence of Jesus without recourse to a misleading metaphor like the resurrection. For example, in 1 Corinthians 5:3 Paul says, "Though absent in body I am present in spirit" (RSV). Now they could have said exactly the same thing about the deceased Jesus, that he was still present in spirit among them. In fact, in the doctrine of the Holy Spirit of Christ they had a theologically rich and profound way of talking about Christ's continuing

3. Ben Witherington III, "Birth of Jesus," in *Dictionary of Jesus and the Gospels*, ed. Joel B. Green, Scot McKnight, and I. Howard Marshall (Downers Grove, Ill.: Inter-Varsity, 1992), 70.

4. Raymond E. Brown, *The Virginal Conception and Bodily Resurrection of Jesus* (New York: Paulist, 1973), 70 n. 121. Brown continues, "Ambiguity arises only about the kind of body involved (earthly, celestial, etc.)."

5. "That *is* the resurrection, the continuing presence in a continuing community of the past Jesus in a radically new and transcendental [sic] mode of present and future existence" (John Dominic Crossan, *The Historical Jesus: The Life of a Mediterranean Jewish Peasant* [San Francisco: Harper, 1991], 404).

presence without all this misleading terminology of resurrection from the dead. But they weren't content to assert merely Christ's spiritual presence with them; they believed that Christ was literally, bodily, physically raised from the dead. In any case, all of this is somewhat academic because we saw in my first contention that the majority of scholars do agree that the burial by Joseph of Arimathea, the discovery of the empty tomb, the appearances of Jesus, and the origin of the disciples' belief are historical facts. They're not metaphors. Responsible historians must explain these facts. The best explanation, I think, is that Jesus rose from the dead.

Now what about Dr. Crossan's bifurcation between the Jesus of history and the Christ of faith? I submit to you that this is simply a pseudodistinction. If one makes this distinction, there are no objective constraints on who or what the Christ of faith is. Whom are we talking about as this "Christ of faith"? The Christ of National Socialist Germany or the Christ of Catholic Ireland? The Christ of Mormons or of Jehovah's Witnesses? The Christ of Jim Jones or of David Koresh? This question is crucial. By making a dichotomy between the historical Jesus and the Christ of faith, Dr. Crossan has no way to determine objectively who the Christ of faith is. But this is a question that we cannot avoid. As Dr. Crossan himself writes, "*Reason* and *revelation*, or history and faith, . . . cannot contradict each other. . . . In theory revelation is superior to reason, in practice reason is usually the final judge. Otherwise, we have no way to evaluate a Jonestown or a Waco situation before it is too late."[6]

6. John Dominic Crossan, *Who Killed Jesus?* (San Francisco: Harper, 1995), 214. Elsewhere he rightly asks, "Is it not morally necessary, especially in our world of docudramas, conspiracy theories, and denials of the Holocaust to distinguish within narrative between fact and fiction, story and history? It is often difficult to do so. Is it not always morally necessary to try?" (John Dominic Crossan, "The Challenge of Christmas: Two Views," *Christian Century*, 15 December 1993, 1280). Yes, we must try, and that is why the Christ of faith must not be loosed from the Jesus of history. Dr. Crossan himself recognizes the problem occasioned by this divorce. In response to the question "Would it be fair to conclude from what you've said that Jesus is not decisive for Christian faith?" he responds, "We touch here on a much wider question. Is the historical Jesus in any way a criterion for Christian faith? . . . I would like to see the debate reopened on a theological level because I think it would force Christian theology to answer the question it never has: What does Jesus have to do with Christ? Does Jesus help us decide between Christs? Maybe, of course, it is already too late" (Crossan, *Historical Jesus*, 1203–4). It is, however, Dr. Crossan's own view, not Christian theology, which has failed to answer that question satisfactorily.

The fact is that we have to be able to critically evaluate proposed Christs of faith by how they measure up to the Jesus of history; otherwise, we may wind up sanctioning Auschwitz or Jonestown. But Dr. Crossan has no objective constraints on the Christ of faith. For him the Christ of faith is whatever one wants him to be.

But then we can ask further, "Why stop with Christ? Why not adopt a non-Christian myth?" Take the example of Octavius Caesar (Augustus). Dr. Crossan writes, "Jesus' divine origins are just as fictional or mythological as those of Octavius. Neither should be taken literally, *both* must be taken metaphorically. But which metaphor do *you* believe in: Octavius-as-divine or Jesus-as-divine? Where do *you* find your God?"[7] Dr. Crossan provides no criteria for making such a choice. In his view Christ is on a par with Thor, Zeus, and Mercury. There simply isn't any way to decide who is the real Christ of faith.

Finally—and with this I close—why believe in such myths at all? Folks, these are fairy tales. It's Peter Pan theology. Why should you get up on a Sunday morning and go worship and pray to somebody who isn't really there? It seems to me that unless the Jesus of history is the Christ of faith, this whole enterprise is irrational, and we might just as well stay home and forget about it.

7. Crossan, "Challenge of Christmas," 1275.

4

John Dominic Crossan's Rebuttal

Let me begin with the question of naturalism and miracles. I've been to Lourdes in France and to Fatima in Portugal—Roman Catholic healing shrines of the Virgin Mary, and I think I really was there as a pilgrim, not just a tourist. I've also been to Epidaurus in Greece and Pergamum in Turkey, which were healing shrines of the pagan god Asklepios. I went there as a tourist. But at both the Catholic and pagan shrines the miracles were remarkably the same. And in both cases I believe that healings did happen.

It is true that at Lourdes, for example, you see many crutches, but you see no wooden legs or empty coffins. It is clear, then, that certain people with certain diseases can be healed under certain circumstances. It is as sure as anything that under certain circumstances and with certain diseases faith heals, which is exactly what Jesus kept saying in the Gospels: "Your faith has healed you." Is that naturalism? If I find something that I cannot explain, I simply say I cannot explain it (which is, if electronics is thrown in, at least 98 percent of the time). And even when I can explain something, it's only my interpretation. The proper answer when confronted with the unexplainable is, "I don't know how that happened. That's a marvel." But this is my theological belief, not naturalism.

In my view the supernatural *always* (at least till this is disproved for me) operates through the screen of the natural. The supernatural is like the beating heart of the natural. It does not come seeping through cracks every now and then, so we can see it. It is always there—but we very seldom see it. So when somebody tells me that such and such happened and it's a miracle, I would never mock, because at that moment that person through faith saw a glimpse of the permanent presence of the supernatural. I might not see it there. Our group might not see it there. But it's there all the time for us to see.

Miracles are acts of faith which say, "Here the supernatural, which is permanently present, is made, as it were, visible to us." That is how I understand miracles. That is not naturalism. It is a belief that the supernatural never forces faith. Maybe that's the blunt way to put it. There's always an out. God never forces faith. One can always say, "It was just chance; it was just luck; it was just a story, or whatever."

I would also disagree with Dr. Craig when he uses the term *majority*. I don't use "majority" quite the way he does. I think it's the job of a scholar to take on the majority every now and then. And if everyone laughs, and if a hundred years from now they're still laughing, then I guess the scholar was wrong. But there is no consensus unless some people every now and then stick their necks way out against the majority and see what happens.

I do not think, however, that Dr. Craig is right—factually right—to assert that a majority of New Testament scholars say that Jesus claimed he was God. I don't think that's correct. I'm not even certain a majority of New Testament scholars say Jesus claimed he was Messiah. What he himself personally claimed is a different matter from what others claimed. Now the majority clearly say that what Jesus talked about was, as the Paternoster says, the kingdom of God (or God's will for the earth). This might be an extraordinary notion, but Jesus might, then, have been more interested in God than he was in himself.

With regard to the resurrection and 1 Corinthians 15, Dr. Craig is quite right that there was no belief in an individual resurrection in Judaism. The Jews could imagine an Elijah taken up to heaven, but that's not quite the same thing. Among certain elements within first-century Judaism (the Pharisees especially) there was a belief in a general resurrection. So when Paul argues in 1 Corinthians 15, "If Jesus is not raised, there's no general resurrection; and if there's no general resurrection, Jesus is not raised," that is the same as saying, "Jesus is the firstfruits of them that sleep." In plain language, the general resurrection has begun with Jesus. Now that's a metaphor. Firstfruits is a reference to the beginning of the harvest. I don't know what Paul, were he here today, would say if we asked him, "Paul, it's two thousand years later; do you still think that's the best way to put it? Or do you think there might be a better way to explain the fact that Christians for two thousand years have experienced the continuing salvific, powerful presence of Christ in their lives? That is a fact, unless we Christians are all liars. How do you explain that fact? Is resurrection still the best way if there's a two-thousand-year gap between the firstfruits and the rest of the harvest?"

A related difficulty occurs where Paul is pushed to describe a resurrected body; he says it is a spiritual body. I do not have a clue what that means. I know what a physical body is. I know what a spirit is. But I don't know what a spiritual body is. I'm not mocking Paul; in fact, I think what he wants to say is absolutely true. He wants to say, "When I speak of the resurrected Jesus, I'm talking about the same Jesus. Everything about Jesus—not just his spirit or his memories or his words, but the same Jesus that was there in the hills of Galilee—is now present and available on the wharves of Corinth. Not just his words, not just his memory, but everything—it's the same Jesus in a totally different mode of existence." So if I were a docker at Corinth listening to Paul's speaking about the resurrection, I wouldn't say, "Okay, Paul, I get it. I believe you. Somebody saw it; you heard it; you're telling me; I believe it." The docker at Corinth believed in the resurrection because, having heard Paul, he was able to experience the empowering presence of Christ in his own life. Resurrection was the way Paul explained it. But the fact was the presence of Christ and the experience thereof. Without that, there is no Christianity. Paul is perfectly right: without that, it's all over. That is what the resurrection means for me—those two things: totally the same Jesus in a totally different mode of being.

Dr. Craig asks why we should believe in a metaphor. We never believe in anything else. We don't need faith for facts. If I were to say to you, "I don't believe in America anymore," you would know immediately that I'm not saying, "I don't think there's a land mass between the borders of Canada and Mexico." I must mean I don't believe in America as the land of opportunity, the land of justice, the land of fairness, the land of the free and the home of the brave, or whatever. It is for metaphors that we live and die—for nothing else. We don't really die for facts. We die for a way of seeing a fact, and that is called a metaphor. In other words, my answer is that we believe in metaphors because there's nothing else to believe in. But we do make choices about the metaphors in which we believe.

47

5

Dialogue

William F. Buckley Jr., John Dominic Crossan, and William Lane Craig

Buckley: We have happily survived the evening so far. Let's see if we can do it for the balance of the hour. I'll begin by asking a couple of questions, the first of which is directed to Dr. Crossan.

Now intending no incivility, I heard you several times refer to yourself as a Christian. This raises a question of definition about which I'm not secure. When I wrote my first book, reaching for the widest, most latitudinarian definition of Christianity, I turned to Reinhold Niebuhr, who said, "There is one thing that in order to be a Christian, one requires a commitment on, and that is that Jesus was other than just a man." Now if you're redefining Christianity, by what authority has this happened?

Crossan: Well there's been no puff of smoke yet, you noticed! So as of now, I'm one up! All right, when I say Jesus was human and divine, "divine" is for me an act of faith. It's not a statement of fact as "Jesus was human" is. That is open to anyone in public discourse. "Jesus is divine" is a statement made by Christians. It means that I, the Christian speaking, find God in Jesus. I do not find God somewhere else. Somebody else may find God somewhere else, but I do not. That's what it means to be a Christian.

Buckley: Wait a minute. We're not talking about comparative religions here. I want to know why it is that you call yourself a Christian. Why don't you say, "Christ—whoever he was—said some interesting things, and to the extent that I have an affinity for what he said, I will call myself a Christian"? But I don't think this makes you a Christian under any formal definition. That's why I really don't know quite what you're doing here under these auspices.

And, incidentally, since we're talking about metaphors, *I* am a puff of smoke!

Crossan: Ah. You brought up the puff of smoke. Let me back up a little bit. We are talking about comparative religion, Mr. Buckley. We really are. There are other religions out there . . .

Buckley: No, we're talking about Christianity.

Crossan: Let me finish. I understand that other people find God elsewhere. To be a Christian for me says that I find God, I experience the presence of God, in Jesus of Nazareth and not somewhere else. That's what it means to be a Christian. Now we presume a group is saying that, not just an individual.

Buckley: But your interest in Christ, I take it, has something to do with the fact that he uttered certain homilies that you find fetching.

Crossan: That would not be my way of putting it. I'm interested in more than just a couple of words. I don't know if there was anything particularly new in what he said. I'm interested in a life—an entire life consummated by a death. That's what's important for me. Of course, he said certain things. He had a vision and a program, and for that vision and that program he was executed. If he did not do that, I wouldn't even know who he was.

Craig: Could I jump in here and press a point?

Buckley: Sure.

Craig: This distinction that you make between statements of faith and statements of fact troubles me. I would like to know, for you, what about the statement that God exists? Is that a statement of faith or fact?

Crossan: It's a statement of faith for all those who make it.

Craig: So in your view, then, factually speaking, it is not true that God exists.

Crossan: That would not be a nice way to put it. Let me put it this way to you. What I'm saying here is that we must take faith se-

49

riously. Understand that Dr. Craig wants to equate faith and fact. There are people in the world who do not believe God exists. I understand that. I happen to think they're wrong, but that does not make it any less an act of faith. They are just putting their faith in something else.

Buckley: But is God omnipotent?

Crossan: In the sense in which you would use the word—that he would use his power to force his will? God does not seem to use omnipotence the way I would use it. If I were omnipotent, I would probably tend to abuse it, to make certain that I got my way.

Buckley: Well, if God is omnipotent, then he can interrupt the natural order, can't he?

Crossan: Can? If we're talking on the level of "can," I probably will not say a single thing about what God can or cannot do. I will make a statement about what I find God doing. I said I find, for example, people are healed by faith. If Roman Catholics were to use that as an argument that only their faith heals (look at Fatima and Lourdes, for example), I would not be able to accept that. God has built healing, if you will, into the universe, for which I thank God.

Craig: But if the existence of God is a statement of faith, not a statement of fact, that means that God's existence is simply an interpretive construct that a particular human mind—a believer—puts onto the universe. But in and of itself the universe is without such a being as God. That is, that's simply an interpretation that a believer puts on it. It seems to me that, independent of human consciousness, your worldview is actually atheistic, and that religion is simply an interpretive framework that individual people put on the world, but none of it is factually, objectively true.

Buckley: Another one of his metaphors.

Craig: Exactly! God himself is a metaphor.

Buckley: "God is a nice thought" is really what you are saying.

Crossan: All right. Well, God is a better thought than some other ones that I know of. No, I would say what you're trying to do is imagine the world without us. Now unfortunately, I can't do

50

that. If you were to ask me (which is just what you did) to abstract from faith how God would be if no human beings existed, that's like asking me, "Would I be annoyed if I hadn't been conceived?" I really don't know how to answer that question.

Craig: Sure you do!

Crossan: Wait a minute! We know God only as God has revealed God to us; that's all we could ever know in any religion.

Craig: During the Jurassic age, when there were no human beings, did God exist?

Crossan: Meaningless question.

Craig: But surely that's not a meaningless question. It's a factual question. Was there a being who was the Creator and Sustainer of the universe during that period of time when no human beings existed? It seems to me that in your view you'd have to say no.

Crossan: Well, I would probably prefer to say no because what you're doing is trying to put yourself in the position of God and ask, "How is God apart from revelation? How is God apart from faith?" I don't know if you can do that. You can do it, I suppose, but I don't know if it really has any point.

Buckley: Dr. Craig, let me ask you to answer concretely a question raised by Dr. Crossan. He says he can't conceive of a spiritual body.

Craig: I think that that's a misunderstanding of what Paul is talking about in 1 Corinthians 15. I think that we have the clue to his meaning in the same letter in the second chapter, where he makes the contrast between the spiritual man and the natural man. Clearly there the "natural man" does not mean "material, physical, extended, tangible man." It means "man under the domination of the natural human nature." And the "spiritual man" doesn't mean "immaterial, invisible, unextended, intangible man." "Spiritual man" there means "a person under the domination and control of the Holy Spirit"—in the same sense that we might say that our pastor is a very spiritual man.

And then when we come to the fifteenth chapter, Paul uses the same vocabulary to contrast the natural body with the resurrection body. He's not talking there about *substance*—what bodies are made out of. He's talking about their *orientation,* so that it's a contrast between, on the one hand, the body that is now dominated by human sin and susceptible to corruption and mortality, and, on the other, the body that will be immortal, incorruptible, free from the effects of sin, and under the complete control of God's Holy Spirit. It's not a contrast between materiality and immateriality; it's a contrast between orientations. So it seems to me that for Paul to talk about a spiritual body as some sort of invisible, unextended, immaterial, intangible body would have simply been a contradiction in terms. He's talking about a real physical body under the domination and control of the Holy Spirit.

Buckley: Dr. Crossan.

Crossan: So in other words, before Jesus' resurrection, his body was under the control of natural forces, sin, and all the rest of that stuff?

Craig: Well, Paul is talking there, as you know, about the general resurrection.

Crossan: Now we're talking about the fifteenth chapter. You made the comparison . . .

Craig: Right. And he's talking there about the general resurrection of the dead, and he's comparing our feeble human nature which is sinful . . .

Crossan: Including Jesus'?

Craig: Well, he doesn't say that Jesus had that kind of natural body. He is talking about the general resurrection there. So he is not asserting that Jesus was dominated by sinful human nature. He's talking about our present bodies in light of our future resurrection. But the main point there is that the contrast he's drawing is not one of substance, but orientation. Even if he were talking about some sort of immaterial body, the point is that that body would be the result of the transformation of the remains of the earthly body in the ground. The body that is sown, he says, will be raised. It's clearly a literal resurrection of the remains of the person in the grave.

Buckley: Yes, but let me ask you this. Is there any sense in which Paul could have spoken or written those words metaphorically? When he said, "If Christ is not risen, then all is in vain," he didn't mean "risen in our estimation," did he?

Craig: No, of course not.

Buckley: He didn't mean "rise" in the sense of "creating more followers." He meant "rise from the dead."

Craig: Right. And, Dr. Crossan, in your work you virtually say that. You say that Paul is arguing there for a bodily resurrection, which is the firstfruits of the general resurrection of the dead, which was certainly literal in Jewish thinking.[1] Paul was a Pharisee. He believed in a literal, physical, general resurrection of the dead. And he thought that in Christ it had begun. So he's not talking about a metaphor there.

Crossan: No, but it is a little bit more complicated than that. When Paul is pushed, he goes straight into a metaphor. You mentioned it. The seed is sown in the ground. Now it's the same seed but something totally different comes up: same seed, totally different ear of barley or whatever. If you were to say to Paul, "All right, Paul, we have people now who are dying before the general resurrection; their bodies are moldering into dust. Would it make any difference, Paul, if those bodies simply disappeared, and instead of their old selves being put back together by divine power, there were a totally new divine body beyond our human understanding? So wouldn't that apply to Jesus'? Would it make a difference, Paul, if the body that Jesus once had, like the bodies you and I have, were simply like the seed, and that whatever happened to it down there is God's business?"

Buckley: But that's really a high form of revisionism. I mean I wouldn't say to Shakespeare, "What would you say about Hamlet if I gave you another chance?"

Crossan: Why not? That would be a marvelous question. Why not?

---

1. John Dominic Crossan, "The Historical Jesus in Earliest Christianity," in *Jesus and Faith,* ed. Robert Ludwig and Jeffrey Carlson (Maryknoll, N.Y.: Orbis, 1994), 7–8.

Buckley: I mean, the fact of the matter is that those were Paul's words. The understanding that they communicated was generally accepted, is generally accepted, will be generally accepted because we know that the gates of hell will not prevail against us. But my question is, Why do you insist on this mad pursuit of the metaphorical meaning to resist the meaning which occurs to us all as reasonable given the historical circumstances as corroborated by the majority of scholars?

Crossan: "Corroborated by the majority of scholars"? There are a few . . .

Buckley: You don't like the majority, I know.

Crossan: Right.

Buckley: You like the few.

Crossan: Yes, I like the few. God's always on the side of the few, Mr. Buckley. You know that.

Buckley: Yes. This consensus that you promised us might materialize a hundred years from now—why has it not materialized already? In fact, it has materialized. At what point do you just do something else?

Crossan: All right. Let's hold Paul for the moment and turn to the stories at the end of the Gospels because this is very important for me. As I read the stories of the crucifixion, nobody has Jesus crucified anywhere except in Jerusalem. That's fairly much set. There are differences in the stories, but the date and time are the same.

　　Nobody gets it wrong. They get the right country, right place, right governor. But when you get to something which would seem to be more important, such as the great final meeting of Jesus and his disciples to give them their worldwide mandate, you find that, for example, in Matthew's Gospel they are on a mountain in Galilee. This is where their mission should begin because Jesus began on a mountain in Galilee with the great Sermon on the Mount. So where else should it be but on a mountain in Galilee that Jesus says, "Go, therefore, and teach all nations"? That's Matthew. When you get to Luke, it all depends. In Luke's Gospel, it's in the upper room. In the Acts of the Apostles, it's out on the Mount of Olives. In John, it is in the upper room. They seem totally free to locate in time and space and detail Jesus' last dramatic meeting with the disciples, which is crucial for the whole future of the church. That's why it's a metaphor.

Buckley: Handle that, Dr. Craig. Is that a problem?

Craig: Dr. Crossan, you seem to be assuming that these accounts are all attempting to narrate the same appearance or the same event, and that's certainly not the case. We have in the case of the appearance to the Twelve multiple, independent attestation, which in your thinking is the key criterion for historical authenticity. We have independent narratives of this event in Luke and in John. Both of them locate it in the upper room in Jerusalem. Then you have it attested by Paul in 1 Corinthians 15. So the appearance to the Twelve, it seems to me, is very well attested—even the location of it, which I regard as a secondary detail and not so important. Regarding the other appearances, it's conceivable, for example, that the appearance on the mountain in Galilee could have been the appearance to the five hundred brethren. It is the same appearance that Mark refers to in the sixteenth chapter of his book. So it doesn't seem to me that there's a diversity that's very troubling.

Crossan: Well, maybe that's because you didn't spend so many years studying it. It is troubling. It really is troubling. To start with Mark, that Gospel ends with an empty tomb and no story of Jesus' apparition. "He goes before you into Galilee; there you will see him as the Lord." Mark doesn't tell the story. And an interpretation of that is that Mark is writing in the context of the Jewish war; because Jesus didn't come to help his beleaguered followers, Mark wants to avoid any mention of apparitions.

Craig: But see? This is based on your peculiar views about Mark—

Crossan: No, no, no.

Craig: That in Mark there are no predictions of resurrection appearances but only of the second coming of Jesus. This is just wrong. In Mark 16:7 and 14:28 there are references to resurrection appearances in Galilee.

Crossan: Does Mark end the story without telling of any resurrection appearances?

Craig: Yes, unless you think the ending has been lost. But I would agree. He simply foreshadows these appearances.

Crossan: So Matthew now is following Mark; when Matthew writes, you can track his following Mark to exactly the point where Mark stops.

Craig: Yes.

Crossan: Then he has Jesus stop the women who in Mark are running away out of fear. He repeats the message to go into Galilee, and then you have the final meeting there.

Craig: Yes.

Crossan: When I read the stories in Luke and John (and I quite agree with you on the upper room), the problem that comes to me is that what we have here is a stream of tradition. That is my problem. It's Mark into Matthew into Luke (and for many scholars) into John. I would put myself into that process: I have a stream of tradition. I don't have a divergence of witnesses at all.

Buckley: Let me ask you something, Dr. Craig. Earlier on, Dr. Crossan said that if a tablet is discovered that establishes this or that about Mark's chronology, then he will retreat from his present position and start again. But let me ask you this. Is it your sense of revelation that the world will never have an exact transcript of the resurrection, by which I mean, Is it ruled out that something like the Shroud of Turin will give us a scientific verification of what we accept as revelation and as historical testimony?

Craig: I wouldn't rule that out a priori. I think it would be presumptuous to rule that sort of thing out. I think any particular case should be taken on its own merits.

Buckley: Well, the merits would certainly be in favor of God disclosing to Dr. Crossan that Jesus really did rise again. So why do you say "on the basis of its merits"? It's obviously meritorious.

But what I'm asking is: Is there anything in your understanding of the Christian statement that says Christ and God moved thus far and no further because they want there always to be some sort of a bridge between revelation and faith?

Craig: Here you're asking me a theological question. I certainly think that God respects the freedom of the will that he has given to human beings; he doesn't overpower them in a sort of divine rape by such an overwhelming display of his glory and power that we are left powerless but to believe. Pascal, the great French physicist and philosopher, quite rightly said that God has given evidence which is sufficiently clear for those with an open mind and an open heart, but which is sufficiently vague so as not to compel those whose hearts are closed.

Buckley: Well, the faith of Pascal was also prudent, wasn't it? He said, "Since I can't absolutely say which way it is, I'd better believe; otherwise, I might get into trouble."

Craig: Yes, the famous Wager Argument—though if you read the rest of his *Apology*, Pascal was also committed to the historical evidences for the resurrection of Jesus and the claims of Christ. This was a part of French apologetic literature at that time, and this was going to be a part of Pascal's *Apology* as well.

Buckley: Yes, but Dr. Crossan raises a very interesting point. He says, "Look. People in fact do get healed by autohypnosis and other means. So why don't we simply agree that what happens at Fatima is no different from what happened at some of the mythic places in Greece?" Now I ask you the question: Is it your understanding that Christianity will deny us what you call blatant demonstration of its validity?

Craig: No, I don't think so. It seems to me that the resurrection, for example, is a miracle which cannot be explained by any stretch of the imagination as being the result of psychosomatic processes.

Buckley: But it's being challenged right now as not having happened. Now, therefore, I guess my question is: Can we reasonably expect a renewed documentation by God of his existence and the divinity of his Son?

Craig: I personally think that God has given evidence which is sufficiently clear for us to already repose confident faith in the resurrection of Jesus. And I have to say that in reading Dr. Crossan's work in preparation for this debate, my belief in the historicity of the resurrection has been strengthened because of the extreme, desperate alternatives to which Dr. Crossan has to go in order to deny it.

Crossan: Just to make it accurate, I am not denying the resurrection. You just don't like my definition of resurrection.

Craig: Well, you're denying it as a historical fact.

Buckley: Let me ask this, Dr. Crossan: In affirming your belief in God, are you, in fact, excluding alternatives to that belief as less plausible than it? Do you believe in God simply because there is revelation, or because there is induction or deduction? Which epistemological processes lead you to affirm belief in God?

Crossan: I don't think it was an epistemological process. It would probably be phony to try to say I argued myself by some logic into belief in God. I really didn't. I think that it was probably that I grew up with it as part of the very fabric of my being. I've never seen any reason to challenge it. I've never seen any argument persuading me against it. But I don't think I really argued myself into it by logic.

Buckley: Well, you grew up thinking that Jesus had been resurrected, and you got over that. You have recuperative powers.

Crossan: No, I got over a *definition* of the resurrection. That's what I got over.

Buckley: You were telling us why you believe in God, having told us earlier that God does not ever speak to us through the kind of revelation that is commonly accepted as such—miracles, for instance.

Crossan: No. I think it would be very simple, for example, if there were a voice that said, "This is God speaking" (in English, I presume, for an American audience). "I'm now going to raise anyone who doesn't believe me twenty-five feet off the ground." Then certain people go up twenty-five feet. "Now do you believe?" And anyone who says no then drops. That would be very easy; I mean, it's the way I think I'd do it if I had that sort of power, and people kept saying something I really disagreed with.

Craig: But you would be coercing belief in that case.

Crossan: Of course! That's why God never does it—not that God can't. God never does it—not by miracle or anything else.

Buckley: Well, Christ did to Thomas something of that nature, did he not?

Crossan: What happens there is that you have somebody who wants—excuse me—proof of your type of resurrection, and he wants to go touchy-feely on the wounds, which is about as literal as you can get. What he's told by Jesus in John's Gospel is, "Blessed are those who have not seen yet believe." What we are talking about there is a resurrection that you can see and feel.

Buckley: Did Christ intend to instruct us or to tip off his apostles that there would be no future demonstration of his divinity as undeniable as what he did for Thomas? Is that what you understand him to have been telling us?

Crossan: No. The example of Thomas is a clear statement that it is not blessed to seek signs or proofs of literal resurrection. In fact, it's cursed.

Craig: I think that the reason that Jesus upbraids Thomas in that story is that Thomas failed to believe on the basis of the apostolic testimony that Jesus was risen. Jesus is not saying, "Thomas, it's blessed to make irrational leaps of faith." He's saying, "You should have believed on the basis of the credible testimony of the other apostles, the eyewitnesses, that I was risen." Similarly, John's readers, though geographically or chronologically removed from the events of the empty tomb and the resurrection appearances, ought to believe on the basis of the apostolic testimony recorded in John's Gospel that Jesus is risen from the dead.

Buckley: This tells us, does it not, that Jesus considered the documentation of his divinity as conclusive? He was distinguishing between those who saw and those who would have to believe without seeing. Those who saw were people who could give testimony to his resurrection.

Craig: I think it is certainly John's point of view that we have adequate apostolic testimony to the resurrection of Jesus; and we can confidently believe on that basis, even though we ourselves haven't seen an appearance of Jesus or discovered an empty tomb.

Crossan: But it would be fair to say, though, that there's nothing about hearing apostolic testimony in the Thomas story. It's strictly about seeing. Thomas wants not only to see; he wants to touch.

Craig: Right.

Crossan: He wants to see and touch, and he's called unblessed. And the reason is that he should have been able to believe without seeing. There's nothing mentioned about apostolic testimony. That's really not in there.

Craig: It's in the conclusion in that John says that these signs are written so that you may believe that Jesus is the Christ, the Son of God, and have life through his name (John 20:30–31). That comes on the heels of the Thomas story, and it in effect says that what Thomas failed to do was to believe what the other disciples had told him.

Crossan: But that would mean that everyone afterwards is in exactly the same state. It's not that the first generation, as it were, could see and touch and feel, but we have to get it secondhand. They were in the same position.

Craig: Right. We get it secondhand in the sense that we rely on the records of those who had it firsthand. Otherwise, Jesus would be required to appear to every single person in every generation in the history of mankind, which is absurd.

Crossan: And call them Thomases.

Craig: Yes.

Buckley: Let me ask you this, Dr. Crossan. Do you, as a matter of philosophical exactitude, rule out the possibility that empirical evidence to come fifty or a hundred years from now may completely confute your presuppositions?

Crossan: Oh, that's open every day. I gave you an example. Any day we might find a Gospel—I mean a real Christian Gospel—dated to the year 100 by means that are beyond dispute. And when we examine it, we might say, "Wait a minute! We're totally wrong on Matthew and Luke; we now see a totally different configuration." While it would not touch directly on the resurrection, it could touch, say, on the presupposition that

Mark was used by Matthew and Luke. So it's definitely wide open. This is not only possible; it's even probable.

Buckley: The tenor of what you have said and the profile of your thought make it plain to me that you simply regard as inconceivable that which we accept. Since it's inconceivable, how can you make room philosophically for the advent of evidence that confutes you?

Crossan: I never used the word *inconceivable.* You brought it into the discussion. What I said is that I don't think your view is the best reading of the data we have. I said Matthew and Luke used Mark, and John may have used all three so that we have a stream of tradition issuing from Mark. On this basis I draw certain conclusions about the nature of the stories. That could change.

Craig: Would there be anything, though, Dr. Crossan, that could convince you that Jesus was risen from the dead as a historical fact?

Crossan: I need to make certain of what we're talking about. Let's say we have a situation outside the empty tomb on Easter Sunday morning. If somebody had a videocam, would he have recorded something coming out of the tomb? Is that the type of question?

Craig: I guess what I'm asking, and what I think Mr. Buckley is pushing for, is this: what evidence would it take to convince you? Or are your preconceived ideas about the impossibility of the miraculous and so forth so strong that, in fact, they skew your historical judgment so that such an event could never even be admitted into court?

Crossan: No. I would ask you to go back to my definition of the miraculous. A doctor at Lourdes might admit, "I have absolutely no medical way of explaining what has happened." That is a right statement. Then one has the right to say, "I by faith therefore believe that God has intervened here." But it's a theological presupposition of mine that God does not operate that way. Rather, faith is built into the universe and has been available to pagan Greeks, to Roman Catholics, and probably in the good old days to Communists if they believed Lenin's tomb would cure them—it would probably be about the same percentage. That's built into the universe already.

What would it take to prove to me what you ask? I don't know, unless God changes the universe. I could imagine discovering tomorrow morning that every tree outside my house has moved five feet. That needs some explanation. I don't know the explanation, but I won't immediately presume a miracle.

Buckley: So therefore you're talking about postulates. Bernadette testified after her second vision that Mary had announced herself as the Immaculate Conception. Then Bernadette said, "What's that?" She'd never heard those words. They'd never been spoken in her presence. How would you account for that?

Crossan: I would not be able to account for a revelation of something which could never have been in a person's mind beforehand. Thus, when little Roman Catholic girls—peasant girls in Europe especially—have a vision of somebody and describe it, I would pay a lot of attention if the Hindus were to say, "That's Kali." But as long as the little girls speak of the Virgin Mary (who always wears the same clothes, by the way—blue and white, Mediterranean sky colors), then I know it's a vision. It operates as visions always do.

Craig: This is one of the strongest arguments in favor of the veridicality of the resurrection appearances—namely, that if these were mere hallucinations or trances, they would not contain anything that was not already in the disciples' minds, for hallucinations are mere projections of the mind. But the resurrection appearances differed from the Jewish framework of beliefs in the afterlife in two fundamental ways. First of all, Jesus' resurrection involved the resurrection of an isolated individual before the end of the world, and secondly, it involved a resurrection in the space-time universe, within history. Given the disciples' Jewish presuppositions and beliefs about the afterlife, were they to hallucinate visions of Jesus, they would have seen visions of Jesus in Abraham's bosom (paradise), where Jews believed the souls of the departed righteous went until the general resurrection. And in that case they would never have been led to belief in Jesus' resurrection. They would have, at most, proclaimed the assumption or translation of Jesus into heaven. The fact that they proclaimed the resurrection, contrary to Jewish beliefs and modes of thinking, supports the fact that these appearances were veridical.

Buckley: And they were not challenged by the Sanhedrin.

Crossan: Two points. First of all, "mere hallucinations" is your term, never mine. A vision is not a hallucination. Secondly, it was within the Jewish frame of reference to do exactly what Paul did—to think in terms not of an isolated resurrection, but of the beginning of the general resurrection. It's often said that Paul expected the end of the world to come soon. Paul thought the end of the world had already begun. That's why he argues both ways. If there is no general resurrection, he says, Jesus hasn't risen. And if Jesus hasn't risen, there's no general resurrection.

Craig: But that's clearly a theological construct that was added after the experience of the resurrection appearances. The question is: Given that the disciples' experiences would be hallucinatory or a visionary trance of some sort, would the disciples have hallucinated and believed in *resurrection* appearances of Jesus? And there the answer is no because the disciples didn't have that theological construct already in their minds.

Crossan: Paul persecuted the church. That meant it was doing something to get him mad. He knew enough about Christianity.

Craig: Sure.

Crossan: He wasn't just minding his own business. He knew exactly what he was doing. He was persecuting the church. Then he had a revelation of Jesus—a *vision*, not a hallucination. That vision fit into his Pharisaic understanding of resurrection. Ah! The general resurrection has begun. The end of the world has begun.

Craig: You see, the problem here is you're talking about Paul whereas I'm talking about the original disciples, and you deny that they had any such apparitional experiences.[2]

Crossan: No, that's not what I do. What I say and say very clearly in the book is that the accounts that you have in the last chap-

2. "The risen apparitions are not historical events in the sense of trances or ecstasies, except in the case of Paul" (John Dominic Crossan, *Who Killed Jesus?* [San Francisco: Harper, 1995], 209).

ters of the Gospels are not visions. I take it for granted that people had visions, not just Paul. In the beginning of any religion, people have visions. I would expect them even if there weren't any recorded. But what I'm saying is that when you get the story of Thomas, the story of the race to the tomb between the beloved disciple and Peter, or the two going to Emmaus and meeting the stranger, those are not visions. There's no blinding light. There's no bang or crash that knocks somebody to the ground. There is, however, the presence, and that's what my contention is: there is the experienced presence of a Jesus who is dead and gone and should be out of here. That is what is fundamental for me. Resurrection is one way of explaining or formulating it.

Buckley: You don't deny, obviously, that Paul intended to communicate his own belief—that the end of the world was around the corner?

Craig: I agree with what Dr. Crossan says. He sees Jesus' resurrection as being the firstfruits of the general resurrection. And in that sense we are living in the final age.

Buckley: Of the last judgment?

Craig: Yes, exactly. But the question is: How could the original disciples, if they experienced hallucinations or visions (as you put it) of Jesus, have experienced visions of Jesus as *risen from the dead?* Given their prior Jewish framework and beliefs about the afterlife, that's not the kind of vision they would have projected.

Buckley: There was incongruity between their visions and the established belief-system.

Craig: Right. They didn't believe in a dying or rising Messiah. They didn't believe a resurrection could occur within history. So if they had hallucinations of Jesus brought on by something or other, they would have seen visions of Jesus in paradise and said he'd been assumed up into heaven—but not risen from the dead. A resurrection within history contradicted fundamental Jewish categories of thinking.

Crossan: I disagree, you understand. I do not agree that it contradicts those categories. Paul was a Jew, and he didn't find it was a contradiction to think that Jesus is the firstfruits of the general resurrection.

Craig: I guess I would be repeating myself in saying that is the theological construct put on *after* the experience. The question is, When these men were confronted simply with the crucifixion and death of Jesus, what would they then have hallucinated before having a chance to put a theological reflection on the experience? It certainly wouldn't lead to belief in Jesus' resurrection. I think this trance argument actually supports the historicity of the appearance stories.

Crossan: Okay, let me leave aside for a moment trance, vision, and hallucination. There's another thing that's equally important, and that is the searching of the Scriptures. In the Emmaus story the explanation of the Scriptures precedes the breaking of the bread. What these disciples did was try to understand if the death of Jesus meant he had been completely condemned by God. Their fear was not that the Romans might come after them, but that God might come after them. They went back to their own Scriptures to find out what the will of God was. Could the Elect One, the Holy One, the Messiah die and still be held in God's hands? They searched all over the Jewish Scriptures, and they found that persecution, if not execution, was almost like a job description of being God's elect. Searching the Scriptures is not done in a trance.

Craig: Right. And that came *after* they had experienced resurrection appearances. But let me comment. The faith of the disciples did not lead to the appearances, but it was the appearances which led to their faith; they then searched the Scriptures.

But let me make a further point on the searching of the Scriptures. In your book, Dr. Crossan, you state very clearly that, at most, the passion narrative could have been constructed on the basis of Old Testament stories and motifs, but not the resurrection narratives, because the Old Testament simply doesn't have material to reinterpret and construe in terms of resurrection.[3] Moreover, you point out that it would have taken at least five to ten years to discover the motifs just

---

3. John Dominic Crossan, *Four Other Gospels* (Minneapolis: Winston, 1985), 174.

to construct the passion.[4] And yet in 1 Corinthians 15:3–4 we have Paul's citing a tradition that most scholars would say goes back to within five years after Jesus' death and that includes both the death of Christ and his resurrection according to the Scriptures.[5] This antedates your reckoning of how long it would have taken to discover the scriptural motifs and construct the passion, much less the resurrection.

Buckley: Let alone this evolution of legendary information.

Craig: Oh, yes. There's just not time.

Buckley: How do you handle that one, Doc?

Crossan: I go back to metaphor. Sorry I'm going to ruin your evening. Go back to Emmaus—two people, probably one male and one female (because only one is mentioned by name—it was typical of Mediterranean society not to identify women), leave Jerusalem. It's Easter Sunday morning. Somebody joins them. Now it's not a vision; it's not a hallucination. There is no blinding light. The stranger explains the Scriptures to them. They say later that their hearts were warmed, but they still didn't recognize him. They then invite this person to come in and eat with them. During the meal they recognize Jesus; then he's gone. That for me is a perfect metaphorical summary of the first years of the church—the searching of the Scriptures and the breaking of bread. Jesus is present—not in a vision, not in a trance, not in a hallucination—but in searching the Scriptures and sharing food with strangers.

Craig: One problem with construing the meal at Emmaus as being some sort of symbol of the Eucharist, in which Jesus would be present, is that at the very moment of the bread-breaking Jesus vanishes—which is exactly the opposite of the Eucharistic presence of Christ. What I think is probably being recalled is Jesus' practice of table fellowship with the disciples and others; he invited sinners and outcasts and the unclean to join him in fellowship around the table. This is what is being recalled in the

---

4. John Dominic Crossan, *Jesus: A Revolutionary Biography* (San Francisco: Harper, 1994), 145; idem, "Earliest Christianity," 19.

5. See the discussion in William Lane Craig, *Assessing the New Testament Evidence for the Historicity of the Resurrection of Jesus,* Studies in the Bible and Early Christianity 16 (Lewiston, N.Y.: Edwin Mellen, 1989), 7–19.

Emmaus story. I don't think that it is necessarily some sort of a Eucharistic symbol.

Buckley: Don't we have here the difficulty, Dr. Crossan, that a lot of data in the Gospels don't lead in the proper direction for a prolonged allegory? This is an interesting intellectual gymnastic act, but why should it appeal to us in the absence of data that you don't have? You've acceded all night long to the fact that Dr. Craig has come up with a number of authorities who validate the historical evidence, but you give the impression of having a resistance to it based primarily on your vision of something different.

Crossan: Not really. If Dr. Craig can convince you that I'm an idiosyncratic, off-the-wall, lonely weirdo, then I'm easily dismissed. The trouble is that what I do is to take the principles that are probably accepted by all biblical scholars and actually apply them to the end of the line. Other scholars tend to apply them to the sayings of Jesus, maybe to the deeds of Jesus. "But now let's stay away from the passion," they say, "and let's really stay away from the resurrection." But the same principles do apply there as well.

Buckley: I suppose applying that kind of diligence we could prove that Lincoln shot Booth rather than vice versa.

Crossan: Now could you?

Craig: In an article I wrote for the book *Jesus under Fire*, which deals with Dr. Crossan's view, I've tried to demonstrate that when the criteria of authenticity that scholars use to establish the sayings of Jesus are applied to the resurrection, we can legitimately conclude that the resurrection ought to be regarded as authentic as well.[6]

Buckley: Thank you, Dr. Craig. Ladies and gentlemen, this is almost the end of our debate. We have five minutes from Dr. Craig coming up, five minutes from Dr. Crossan, and then five from me.

---

6. William Lane Craig, "Did Jesus Rise from the Dead?" in *Jesus under Fire*, ed. Michael J. Wilkins and J. P. Moreland (Grand Rapids: Zondervan, 1995), 162–63. Specifically, various facts concerning the resurrection can be established on the basis of the criteria of multiple attestation, dissimilarity, embarrassment, context and expectation, effect, principles of embellishment, and coherence.

6

Closing Statements

William Lane Craig

In 1994 the *Chicago Tribune Magazine* carried an article on Dr. Crossan's views that was entitled "Gospel Truth" with the subtitle "Will Christians Accept a Revolutionary Portrait of Jesus That Is Based on Scholarship, Not on Faith?"[1] As is so typical of media caricatures of Christianity, the article portrayed Dr. Crossan's views as based on scholarship and the biblical view as based on faith. I hope that if there's one thing that you get out of tonight's debate, it will have been that precisely the opposite is the case. It is the biblical view that presents us with a revolutionary portrait of Jesus that is supported by scholarship, whereas the theologically liberal picture of Jesus painted by Dr. Crossan is based sheerly on faith.

In particular, I think we've seen tonight, first, that the real Jesus rose from the dead in confirmation of his radical personal claims to divinity. I argued that Jesus put himself in the place of God, and all Dr. Crossan has said here is, "I'm not sure the majority of critics think that Jesus said he was God." The point, however, is that the majority of critics do believe that Jesus did things by which he put himself in God's place. As Royce Gordon Gruenler says, Jesus is "consciously speaking as the voice of God on matters that belong only to God. . . . The evidence clearly leads us to affirm that Jesus implicitly claims to do what only God can do: to forgive sins. . . . The religious authorities correctly understood his claim to divine authority to forgive sinners, but they interpreted his claims as blasphemous

1. Jeff Lyon, "Gospel Truth: Will Christians Accept a Revolutionary Portrait of Jesus That Is Based on Scholarship, Not on Faith?" *Chicago Tribune Magazine,* 17 July 1994, 9.

and sought his execution."[2] So if Jesus' radical claims are not true, he is literally a blasphemer.

But the resurrection of Jesus vindicates those claims. We noted the facts of (1) the burial by Joseph of Arimathea, (2) the discovery of the empty tomb, (3) the resurrection appearances, and (4) the origin of the disciples' belief. Remarkably, Dr. Crossan hasn't challenged the historicity of any of those facts. And I don't see how he can deny that the resurrection is the best explanation of them.

As for Dr. Crossan's presuppositions, again, remarkably, in tonight's debate he hasn't tried to defend any of them: (1) the priority of the Gospel of Peter, (2) the Secret Gospel of Mark, (3) the inventive community of early Christians. All he said is that he's not a naturalist. Yet he does insist that the supernatural acts only through the natural. That would exclude a priori an event like the resurrection because there is no natural means by which an event like the resurrection could have been brought about. It was painfully obvious in the dialogue time that there is no evidence that could convince Dr. Crossan of the historicity of Jesus' resurrection, for he rules it out of court a priori.

Now if Jesus was not risen from the dead, then it does seem to me that Christianity is just a fairy tale which no rational person should believe. Dr. Crossan's way of defending belief in Christianity apart from the historicity of the resurrection is to say it's metaphorical. But I challenged him to show that the Gospels are a metaphorical genre of literature rather than historical, and he never came back on that point. In particular, we saw that the virgin birth story is not like any story of pagan mythology.

With respect to the resurrection, I showed two things. First, the earliest Christians interpreted the event literally. They saw an empty tomb in its wake. They wondered about what kind of body the resurrection body would be. And, secondly, in any case, my first contention showed that these evidences of the resurrection aren't metaphors; they are real historical facts.

And then, you remember, I challenged Dr. Crossan to show us any constraints that would exist on the Christ of faith. Why not the Nazi Christ? Why not the Jim Jones Christ or the David Koresh Christ? And Dr. Crossan hasn't yet answered that question. Then I

---

2. Royce Gordon Gruenler, *New Approaches to Jesus and the Gospels* (Grand Rapids: Baker, 1982), 46, 59, 49.

asked, "Why not believe a non-Christian myth? Why not believe in Thor or Zeus or Octavius?" And he hasn't given any criteria for excluding non-Christian myths.

Finally, I asked, "Why believe in myths at all?" He replied, "Well, we have nothing but myths." Not at all! I think we've seen tonight that we have good historical facts as the foundation for our faith as Christians. And I want to encourage you, if you've never looked into this yourself, to begin to read the New Testament and ask yourself, "Could this really be true? Could Jesus really be the Son of God, risen from the dead, and come for my salvation?" When I began to look into this as a non-Christian teenager, I found that it was true, and it changed my life. And I believe that if you look into it with an open heart and an open mind, these facts can change your life as well.

John Dominic Crossan

I get to go last; so I get to be as mean as I want, and I can't be rebutted!

If you have learned anything here tonight, it is "Don't believe everything you read in the *Chicago Tribune!*"

When I was invited to participate in this debate, I agreed because I think religions are talking to one another in this ecumenical age. But the ultimate ecumenism will be when liberal Christians talk to conservative Christians. If I have done anything to foster that, it was good to have been here. I did not think I would change Dr. Craig's mind. I did not think I would convert him. And I don't know how one wins a religious debate. There's no election afterwards to determine who was right and who was wrong. So I didn't expect to convert anyone or to win anyone over. I wanted to let you hear a conservative viewpoint with its own integrity and its own respect; to let you hear a liberal or (maybe) radical viewpoint with its own integrity and its own respect; and to ask you, "What are you going to do about the fact that both of us are within Christendom or—to Mr. Buckley's displeasure—that I claim to be a Christian despite such weird ideas?"

I would hope that this sort of debate/dialogue can go on. We've managed to do it tonight without impugning one another's competence or motivation, without calling one another names. We have simply tried to explain our ideas to each other. We've managed not to talk against one another or just about one another in the other's absence. We have met face to face. Maybe if we can continue that, then, if I may borrow the title of a recent novel, instead of being "brothers no more" or brothers and sisters no more, we will be sisters and brothers—once again—in Christ.

71

William F. Buckley Jr.

It seems to me that what we continue to discover in life is the restive nature of the human intelligence. John Stuart Mill said over a hundred years ago, "As long as a single person believes something, we cannot consider that question closed." Now this is a theory of knowledge with which I do not agree because it is clear to me that we will always find one person who disputes almost any given proposition: the flat-earthers or the grassy-knollers who won't be convinced that Mr. Kennedy was killed by his assassin. And we have a sort of grassy-knoll Christianity now in which people are seeking other answers for certain questions that have been considered closed. I don't believe that progress can be made without closing questions, because, if indeed the truth will set us free, then we are to some extent charged (are we not?) with confronting errors and finding an appropriate attitude toward them. It seems to me that there are limits to the civilized sense of curiosity. Whether one should honor one's mother and father, whether one should be true to one's faith or to one's family, or be prepared to make sacrifices, are not questions that ought to be raised every few minutes by some restive intelligence.

The conviction is quite general in the Christian community—and, indeed, in the Jewish community and even within Islam—that on the whole it is much easier to affirm a God and, derivatively, a Christ because many more questions are answered by faith than by skepticism. And, under the circumstances, to find opportunities to engage that restiveness is not really to contribute to that pool of intelligence which marks progress.

Dr. Crossan has, in his patient and ingratiating manner, said that the whole Christian idea (because the whole Christian idea has to do with the divinity of Christ) is really nothing but an evolving legend. Dr. Craig said that there wasn't time for a legend to evolve in the five short years between the crucifixion and the time when the tradition that was handed on to Paul began to speak of it as the most unmistakable event in world history.

As regards evolving legends, I'm reminded of the Darwinian who, inflamed by the evolutionary discoveries that had been so widely circulated since 1859 (in the publication of *The Origin of Species*), was asked in 1870 (finally cornered, they said), "Under the circumstances, what do you think about the evolution of Christianity? Is it finally destroyed?" He paused for a moment, and he said, "In my judgment God does not cease to exist, because on the whole I find it easier to believe in God than to believe in the evolution into *Hamlet* of a molecular structure of a mutton chop." Similarly, it is much easier to assume (is it not?) that there is a divine transcendent order that has given to our lives what keenness they have and inspired our idealism, and that the risen Christ is the source of that special Christian idealism which brings us together.

Part 2

Responses and Concluding Reflections

7

Responses

What Do Stories about Resurrection(s) Prove?

Robert J. Miller

The debate between William Lane Craig and John Dominic Crossan is about the historical accuracy of the resurrection stories in the Gospels. Craig maintains that these stories are evidence that the resurrection is literally true (that is, that Jesus' corpse came back to life and left the tomb). Crossan believes in Jesus' resurrection, but maintains that the Gospel stories do not provide evidence that the resurrection is historically true in a literal sense.

I agree with Crossan. However, instead of responding directly to Craig's argument, I will step back from it and analyze its format, message, and audience. I take this approach because Craig's message about the resurrection and the way he communicates it to his audience are similar in some very important ways to the message of the Gospels and the way they convey it to their audience. Understanding Craig's method and message can thus clarify our understanding of the meaning of the resurrection stories in the Gospels.

In the first part of my essay I analyze Craig's attempt to persuade us that Jesus' resurrection is a historical fact. I pay special attention to how and for whom this kind of persuasion works. Then I will use these insights to analyze the resurrection stories in the Gospel of Matthew. My aim is to discern what Matthew thought he was doing in telling those stories in just the way he did and how his audience understood them.

Robert J. Miller is associate professor of religion and philosophy at Midway College in Midway, Kentucky.

Apologetics and Outsiders

Craig's central thesis is that the bodily resurrection of Jesus is a fact that can be demonstrated by historical evidence and sound reasoning. According to Craig, we don't really need faith to affirm the resurrection; we need only think clearly and objectively about the evidence and draw unbiased conclusions. Craig's argument is an apology for Jesus' resurrection. The term *apology* here has nothing to do with saying that one is sorry. In the sense the term has here, an apology is a rational defense for a certain belief. In general, an apology for the resurrection is an argument that it is reasonable to believe that Jesus was raised from the dead, though Craig's apology goes beyond this. He not only argues that belief in the resurrection is *a* rational option, he argues that it is the *only* reasonable option, and thus it would be irrational not to believe in it.

Craig presents his apology in a debate with Crossan, which is confusing since Crossan also believes in the resurrection. Two people cannot debate an issue on which they agree. Craig's argument appears to be designed for a debate with someone other than Crossan, someone who does not believe in the resurrection.[1] That is how apologies in general seem to work: they seem to be addressed to outsiders (those who do not share the belief being defended). They look like attempts to persuade others to change their minds and adopt new beliefs. But is this understanding accurate? Are apologies really meant for outsiders? This is an extremely important question. The way we answer it determines how we approach the whole issue of the historical accuracy of the Gospel stories.

For whom are apologies really intended? In this case, the Craig-Crossan debate took place at Moody Memorial Church in Chicago. What percentage of that audience was non-Christian? How many of the listeners were outsiders in the sense that they did not share the belief that Craig defended? And what percentage of the readers of this book published by Baker Book House will be non-

---

1. A major problem in the debate is that Craig seems to assume that Crossan denies the resurrection, an assumption shared by Buckley, who clearly sides with Craig. Craig and Buckley apparently think that Crossan is either confused or dissembling when he affirms his belief in the resurrection. This may be why Craig insists that those who do not believe in the resurrection in exactly the way he does (i.e., literally) have no business being Christians, another sentiment shared by Buckley.

Christian? The answer to all these questions is the same: very, very few, if any at all.

In the few cases when outsiders do read or listen to apologies, they seldom take them seriously (i.e., in the spirit in which they present themselves). Outsiders approach apologies with caution, for the simple reason that apologies ask them to change their beliefs. Most outsiders assume that apologies are greatly biased, that they tell only one side of the story. Outsiders read apologies more often out of curiosity or out of a desire to figure out how to refute them than out of a willingness to give up their own beliefs.[2] (You can check this by asking whether in reading literature from the Hare Krishna movement you would seriously open your heart and mind to the possibility that Krishna is the Supreme Lord of the Universe.)

An Apology for Islam

We can get a feel for how outsiders regard apologetics by briefly considering an apology for a religion other than Christianity. Islam is an interesting case for Christians to consider because both Christians and Muslims believe that their religions originated through the direct intervention of God, through a divine miracle that is unparalleled and unsurpassable. Both believe that God had intervened at various times in the past to reveal his will for humanity, but that those revelations were provisional and incomplete. Both Christians and Muslims believe that God finally intervened with a perfect revelation that gives us everything we need to know to do his will and find salvation. For Christians, this miracle of perfect revelation is the life, death, and resurrection of Jesus. For Muslims, this miracle is the Qur'an revealed through the prophet Muhammad.

Muslim apologists maintain that unbiased consideration of the evidence confirms the belief that Islam was established by God through the miracle of the Qur'an. Although this miracle was not in itself public (there was nothing to see), reason can nonetheless confirm it by assessing its effects. That is, the divine origin of the Qur'an

---

2. Outsiders assume (usually correctly) that the apologist is not willing to give up *his* beliefs. Outsiders thus suspect (again usually correctly) that the apologist is, in effect, saying to them, "I'm asking you to be more open-minded than I am," even if an apologist would never be so crude in his actual wording.

is the only rational explanation for a number of otherwise inexplicable realities.

First, the Qur'an is completely inerrant. It contains no contradictions and no errors of any kind, not even scientific ones. In fact, some of its descriptions of natural phenomena are consistent with scientific discoveries made centuries after Muhammad.

Second, the Qur'an is unsurpassed in the beauty of its poetry and the grandeur of its language (which can be fully appreciated only in Arabic). The Qur'an even challenges those who do not believe in its divine origin to create a chapter, or even one verse, that compares with it. The Qur'an is a literary masterpiece, yet Muhammad was uneducated and illiterate.

Third, the Qur'an has great spiritual power. It had a profound effect on those who first heard it, moving them deeply and leading many to immediately convert to Islam.

Fourth, the Qur'an's sublime monotheism and its elevated moral teaching were far ahead of the time and place of its earthly origin. Seventh-century Arabia was a place of deeply rooted polytheism and of rampant violence, widespread vice, and harsh social oppression. The Qur'an's uncompromising monotheism and its demand for social justice and strict personal morality were utterly foreign to its environment.

Finally, Muhammad never wavered in his claim that the Qur'an was from God and not from him. This claim reflects his sincere belief, for Muhammad was neither a liar nor a megalomaniac nor delusional. He was famous for his honesty; even his enemies admired his integrity. Far from being a megalomaniac, his lifestyle was modest and unassuming, and he drew a strict distinction between the times he was relaying revelation and the times he was expressing his own thoughts. Neither was Muhammad delusional. His enormous successes as a social reformer and as a political and military leader amply demonstrate his keen grasp of reality.

Further evidence for the divine origin of Islam is the speed at which it grew in a time and place that were hostile to it. Nothing in the culture of seventh-century Arabia favored Islam's monotheism or its elevated and demanding morality. In fact, there were powerful religious, economic, social, and political forces arrayed against it. Muhammad's first followers in Mecca were cruelly persecuted, and his fledgling community in Medina was attacked by vastly superior military forces. Islam not only survived, but spread so rapidly that by the time of Muhammad's death just two years after his return to Mecca, virtually all of Arabia had embraced Islam.

Please bear in mind that all this is merely the rough sketch of an apology for Islam. A Muslim scholar of Islam (which I am not) could present these ideas and others with much more force and eloquence. Yet even if this apology were laid out with far greater skill than I can manage, how convincing do you think it would be to Christians? How many Christians would it convince that Islam is the religion God intends for all humanity? How seriously does it make you question your beliefs?

Muslim apologists maintain that the Qur'an would not be so inerrant, profound, beautiful, and compelling if God were not its author, and that Islam would not have been accepted by so many so quickly unless it were divinely guided. Muslims find this line of argument utterly convincing. Non-Muslims, however, will not be persuaded, even if they do not know how to explain the admirable qualities of the Qur'an or the impressive growth of early Islam. They will assume that even if they themselves do not know how to refute the apology, there are experts who do. Similarly, many readers of this book are confident that even if they personally cannot answer Crossan's arguments, surely someone like Craig can.

Outsiders seldom read apologies and seldom take them seriously when they do. As for the few non-Christians who do read an apology like Craig's and do give it serious consideration, how many are actually persuaded by it? Again the answer is very, very few, if any at all.[3]

Looking at the Resurrection from the Outside

Having considered how an apology for some other religion looks to us (for the sake of the argument I am assuming that my readers are

3. Of course, there may be a few for whom an apology is persuasive, and for them the difference it makes in their lives is dramatic. Insiders who focus on these rare cases and ignore the rest can get the mistaken impression that apologetics is highly effective. In some cases the apologist himself came to faith this way and so knows the power of apologetics from his own experience. Converts can be very committed evangelists, missionaries, and apologists. Nevertheless, almost no Hindus, Buddhists, Jews, or Muslims (to name only some), nor atheists or agnostics will be persuaded by an apology like Craig's.

Christian), we can round out the process with a "thought experiment." Imagine that you are not a Christian, but that you've come across Craig's apology for the literal historicity of Jesus' resurrection. For whatever reason, you take it seriously and decide to make a careful study of the relevant Gospel stories. As you read the stories about the empty tomb and the appearances, you notice again and again how different they are from Gospel to Gospel. So you construct charts that lay out the similarities and the differences. (See figures 1–3.) What do you make of all the disparity? Perhaps you conclude that the early Christians couldn't keep their stories straight, or that nobody knew what had actually happened. Maybe at one time somebody did, but by the time the Gospels were written the details had become so confused that the actual story was hopelessly lost. Or maybe you would conclude that the differences are indications that the stories were never meant to be taken literally. In any case, the many striking disparities would reinforce your doubts about the historical reliability of the stories.

It is natural for outsiders to focus on differences and the historical problems they create. But what about insiders? Do they grow skeptical when they reflect on all the differences among the resurrection stories? A few might begin to have some doubts, but the vast majority of insiders are not much bothered by the disparities. Insiders seldom notice them; if they do, they do not regard them as real inconsistencies. In fact, some apologists even flip these differences over to *increase* insiders' confidence in the historical reliability of the stories. They do this by arguing that, even with all the disparities, the versions all still agree that some followers of Jesus found his tomb empty.

The point I want to make is that while insiders and outsiders may read the same stories, they will use very different standards in evaluating their historical reliability. Imagine that another religion had a story about how God had worked mighty miracles that demonstrated the truth of that religion. Imagine also that there were several versions of this story and that these versions had numerous discrepancies, inconsistencies, and contradictions. Wouldn't you, a Christian and thus an outsider to this religion, point to those disparities as evidence for the unreliability of the stories? People are naturally more charitably inclined to their own stories than they are to those of outsiders.

Figure 1

Empty-Tomb Stories

	Mark	**Matthew**	**Luke**	**John**
Time	sunrise	before dawn	daybreak	still dark
Persons involved	Mary Magdalene, Mary James's mother, Salome	Mary Magdalene, the other Mary	Mary Magdalene, Mary James's mother, Joanna, other women	Mary Magdalene
Position of the stone	stone already rolled away	stone rolled away by an angel during an earthquake	stone already rolled away	stone already rolled away
Guards	no	yes	no	no
Figures at the tomb	a young man sitting inside the tomb	an angel sitting on the stone outside the tomb	no one at first, then two men	two angels sitting inside the tomb
Message	"Tell the disciples to go to Galilee"	"Tell the disciples to go to Galilee"	"Remember that Jesus told you all this would happen"	——
Reaction	fear	fear and great joy	——	Mary mistakes Jesus for the gardener, but recognizes him when he says her name
Response	the women tell no one	the women tell other disciples	the women tell the apostles (Peter comes to the tomb and sees the linen wrappings)	Mary tells the other disciples

FIGURE 2
Easter Appearance Stories

	Matt. 28:9–10	Luke 24:13–33	Luke 24:34	Luke 24:36–51	John 20:19–23
Persons involved	the women who came to the tomb	two disciples	Simon	the Eleven and others	disciples
Place	between the tomb and hideout	on the road to Emmaus	?	a room in Jerusalem	a room in Jerusalem
Reaction	worship	nonrecognition	?	fear; they mistake Jesus for a ghost; "they disbelieve for joy"	gladness
Confir–mation	——	——	?	Jesus invites them to touch him; he eats fish	Jesus shows them his hands and side
Message	"Tell the disciples to go to Galilee"	(Jesus interprets Scripture)	?	(Jesus interprets Scripture and commissions them to preach repentance and forgiveness in his name)	(conferral of the Holy Spirit and authority to forgive and retain sins)
Con–clusion	——	they recognize him as he breaks bread; he vanishes; they return to Jerusalem	?	Jesus leads them to Bethany and ascends into heaven *(end of Gospel)*	——

FIGURE 3

Post-Easter Appearance Stories

	Matt. 28:16–20	John 20:26–29	John 21	Acts 1:1–11
Time	?	one week later	some time later	over a forty-day period
Persons involved	the Eleven	disciples (including Thomas)	seven disciples	the apostles
Place	a mountain in Galilee	a room in Jerusalem	the Sea of Tiberias	Jerusalem
Reaction	some worship him; some doubt	———	recognition	———
Confirmation	———	Jesus invites Thomas to touch him	———	———
Message	the Great Commission	blessing on those who believe without seeing	feed my lambs (to Peter); discussion of the fate of the beloved disciple	wait for the Holy Spirit; be my witnesses
Conclusion	*(end of Gospel)*	———	*(end of Gospel)*	Jesus ascends into heaven

To consider a specific example, how many non-Mormons take seriously the story about Joseph Smith discovering the golden tablets that contained the Book of Mormon and deciphering them with spectacles made of stone? Non-Mormons find this story unbelievable if not mildly amusing. But most Mormons find it easy to believe, and those few with doubts can overcome them by strengthening their faith through prayer. Why should non-Mormons find the story hard to believe? After all, it is no more implausible than dozens of stories in the Bible (for example, Jonah and the whale) that many Christians believe with no difficulty at all. The difference has very little to do with the stories themselves and a great deal to do with whether one approaches them as an insider or an outsider. To put it a bit crudely perhaps, stories about our miracles are easy to believe because

85

they're true; stories about their miracles are easy to dismiss because they're far-fetched and fictitious.

Why Doesn't Apologetics Succeed?

Why is it that very few, if any, outsiders will be persuaded by Craig's apology? From the way he presents it, we get the impression that he thinks that nobody who is informed, rational, and sincere could disagree with it. So why doesn't it work? There are really only two alternatives: the apology fails to convince either because it is unpersuasive, or because outsiders miss the truth, usually by reasoning incorrectly and drawing the wrong conclusion, or by seeing the truth but not accepting it. In other words, there is a defect either in the apology or in the "apologee," and since few apologists present an argument they believe is defective, they are more or less forced to blame the apologee for failing to see, or to admit, the truth.[4]

The problem with blaming the apologee is that not only is that self-serving, it is also gratuitous. What evidence is there that the apologee is not smart enough to follow the apologist's reasoning, or not sincere enough to want to know the truth, or not honest enough to admit it? The only answer the apologist gives is that if the apologee really were rational and well intentioned, he would agree with the apologist. Needless to say, most people are not impressed by this line of reasoning.

I used to think this way myself when I was a fervent believer in the power of apologetics. I was a philosophy major at a Catholic college. I was utterly convinced not only that Christianity was the one true religion that God intended for all humanity, but also that the Catholic Church was the one true church that Christ intended for all Christians. From my study of Thomas Aquinas and modern Chris-

---

4. This actually happened to me. A few years ago I was having dinner with several seminary professors. One of them, a professor of philosophy, was presenting his arguments for the divinity of Jesus. Like Craig's argument, his was presented as if only irrational people could disagree with it. I found it unpersuasive and asked him why he thought this was. He volunteered that I was informed and intelligent. When I pressed him as to why he thought I nevertheless disagreed with his apology, he replied that the reason might be that I was a sinner. The others at the table were visibly embarrassed, and an awkward silence lasted several long seconds. We moved on to another topic after I admitted being a sinner and then asked him if that made me any different from him.

tian apologists, I clearly saw that the central truths of Christianity (and of Catholicism) could be grasped by reason if only one was sincerely seeking God's truth, was humble enough to accept it, and took the time to inform oneself and follow the arguments.

All of this made perfect sense to me, and none of my teachers or fellow students (all of whom were Catholics) gave me any reason to question it. I tried out various apologetic arguments on my like-minded friends, who found them quite convincing. Occasionally they suggested improvements in my arguments, but none of us doubted the effectiveness of apologetics. The only real puzzle in my mind was this: since the truths of Christianity and Catholicism are so evident, why are they not more universally recognized? I concluded that those outside my religion or my church just did not know or did not understand these apologetic arguments, or that they were not completely sincere about seeking the truth. It amazes me now that I believed this without any feelings of superiority or smugness. I was sincerely grateful to God for the blessing of having been raised in the Christian religion and the one true church, and I prayed for the wisdom and the courage to be able to help others to see the truth as clearly as I did.

This mind-set held together until I went to graduate school at secular universities and got to know people who had different religions. For the first time in my life, I got to know people who took other religions as seriously as I took mine. I knew these people were well educated and highly rational, and I could tell from our conversations that they were sincere. A few were people of great goodness and spiritual depth. Yet none of them was persuaded by my apologetics. It took several years, but gradually I accepted the fact that informed, intelligent, sincere, and spiritual people are almost never persuaded by apologetics to change their core beliefs. Looking back, I can now see that a big reason for this is that most apologists use assumptions that only insiders take for granted. It is usually only from an outsider's perspective that one can see how problematic these assumptions really are.

In summary, apologies almost never reach outsiders. When they do, they are almost never taken seriously; when they are, they are almost never persuasive. So, if the purpose of apologetics is to convince outsiders to adopt new beliefs, then apologies are almost always abject failures. They fail, not because their authors are inept (like Craig, many of them are intelligent thinkers and capable writers), but because it is practically impossible to argue people into giving up their religious beliefs and adopting new ones.

However, there is another, more promising way to evaluate the apologetic genre. We can determine its audience, not by whom it seems to be aimed at, but by who actually reads it. And we can determine its purpose, not by what the author seems to intend, but by how it actually functions. If we proceed like this, we reach two important findings: (1) the audience for an apology is insiders; (2) its function is to support what the audience already believes.

This is nothing new to apologists, who know full well that their audiences are insiders. (Why else would Craig speak at Moody Memorial Church or write for Baker Book House?) So why do apologists write as if they were addressing outsiders? They do that, not because they are mistaken about their audience, but because that is the convention of the apologetic genre. An apt comparison is the genre of the open letter. An open letter may begin, "To the President of the United States," but both author and readers understand that the real audience is the general public. Readers don't think they are reading the president's mail. Everyone knows the difference between an open letter and a personal letter that is leaked to the press. The general public knows the open letter is intended for them, even though it is addressed to the president. Every genre has its own conventions. Authors of fables write about talking animals because that is how fables go, not because anyone thinks that animals really talk.

Acquaintance with the conventions of apologetics makes a difference because it helps us understand what Craig's writing is really about. Since it is meant for insiders, even though it seems to be addressed to outsiders, we have to distinguish its message (that is, its message to its real audience) from its content. Its content is an argument aimed at convincing outsiders that they should believe in the resurrection literally because that is the rational thing to do; indeed, to do otherwise would be irrational. But the message to the real audience is that their belief in Jesus is far more than wishful thinking; it is founded on solid evidence and can be defended by someone with impressive academic credentials against an eloquent detractor. (There is, then, a mismatch in the Crossan-Craig debate. Crossan does not deny the resurrection, though he does deny that the Gospel stories about it are literally true—a position Craig ridicules as "Peter Pan theology.")

The Audience of the Gospels

It should now be clear that in order to understand what a text is really about, we need to take into account who its audience is and how it functions for that audience. Only after we figure out these elements can we make an informed judgment about what the message of the text is. Let's look, as an example, at the resurrection stories in the Gospels.[5] Who is the audience for these stories? What did their authors think they were doing in writing the way they did? And how did these stories function for their audience?

Craig treats the Gospel stories as literal accounts of what really happened. For him these are stories about how faith in the resurrection got started: the earliest Christians believed that Jesus was raised because some of them had actually seen him in his physical body after his death. Craig argues that if people today properly understand these stories, they will conclude that Jesus was physically raised from the dead, and from this they will conclude that Jesus is God. Craig folds these Gospel stories into his own argument, which seems aimed at outsiders but is actually for believers. Craig's argument thus appears to be intended to induce faith, but it actually functions to confirm the faith of those who already believe.

We need to ask: Who is the audience of the Gospels? For whom did the Evangelists write? The answer is clear: the Gospels were written for Christians. They presuppose that their audiences already believe in Jesus. Although a few outsiders may read a Gospel, it is most unlikely that any of them will come to believe in Jesus by reading that text. This is especially so in the case of the resurrection stories. How likely is it that a Jew or a pagan would read one of these stories and then conclude that Jesus has been physically raised from the dead and that therefore he is God? No, the resurrection stories presume a friendly audience, people who already believe that Jesus has risen. The stories presuppose and build on that belief in order to teach about the meaning of Jesus' resurrection and its implications for the Christian life.

---

5. Technically, there are no resurrection narratives in the New Testament. That is, there are no stories that tell of Jesus' coming back to life and emerging from the tomb. All four Gospels have stories about his followers' finding his tomb empty, and three Gospels have stories about Jesus' appearing to his followers after his death. (The Gospel that Mark wrote ended at 16:8 with the women fleeing the tomb—the stories in 16:9–20 were added in the second century.)

The Resurrection of the Righteous Jews

To get specific about what the Evangelists are trying to communicate in the resurrection stories, we need to focus on one specific Gospel as an example. Any one will do, but Matthew is especially appropriate because some features unique to this Gospel give us strong clues as to its author's intentions.

A fascinating peculiarity of Matthew is that he tells of other resurrections in addition to Jesus'. According to Matthew, many righteous Jews were raised from the dead along with Jesus. At the very moment that Jesus died,

> the earth shook, and the rocks were split. The tombs also were opened, and many bodies of the saints who had fallen asleep were raised. After his resurrection they came out of the tombs and entered the holy city and appeared to many. [Matt. 27:51–53 NRSV]

What should we make of this strange story? Did it really happen? And what does it mean?

We need to take a close look at this brief account because it can tell us a great deal about what Matthew thought he was writing and what his audience thought they were reading. The first question we have to tackle is whether this story is historical.

To put it bluntly, there is no good reason to think that this event really happened. For it is mentioned nowhere else—not in another Gospel, not in any other Christian writing, not in the writings of Josephus (a well-informed and meticulous Jewish historian of the time). In most cases it is invalid to conclude that an event did not happen simply because it is mentioned in only one source—after all, lots of things occur that are not recorded even once. But this story is a very special exception to the rule because it narrates what by any measure has to be the most amazing event of all time: large numbers of dead people coming to life and appearing to large numbers of witnesses. It is inconceivable that an event so sensational and of such magnitude would not be noticed by the historians of the day. It's especially inconceivable that no other Christian source would mention it.[6] The

---

6. It is virtually impossible to explain why Paul does not mention this event if it actually happened. In 1 Cor. 15:5–8 Paul emphasizes the reality of Jesus' resurrection by listing those who had experienced the risen Jesus. How could he fail to mention those who had experienced their own resurrections as a result of his? Furthermore,

people who had left their tombs on Easter would have been hugely famous among Christians. A few lucky disciples could claim to have seen the risen Jesus, but these people were even more privileged: they had been raised from the dead along with Jesus. Yet their story left no trace anywhere outside these three short verses in Matthew.

Unless one is committed to belief in the literal historicity of every passage in the Bible, there is no basis for taking Matthew 27:51–53 to be the report of an actual event. Does this mean that Matthew was misinformed or that he was lying? Not at all. Matthew never intended this account to be taken literally. He assumed that his audience would take it symbolically and understand its message accordingly.

What is that message? Two features of this brief narrative furnish clues that would have been clear to Matthew's readers: the earthquake and the way Matthew characterizes those who rise. Both features told Matthew's readers that the death/resurrection of Jesus is the decisive event in salvation history, the event that ushers in the time of the fulfilment of God's plans for humanity. This account has the same message as do twelve others in which Matthew interrupts the Gospel narrative to tell the readers that a certain event fulfils what was foretold by the prophets—that God's promises to Israel are coming true in Jesus, that Jesus (in his birth, life, death, and resurrection) is the culmination of Israel's hopes and of God's plans for his people.

One feature in 27:51–53 that conveys Matthew's message is how he describes those who are raised from the dead: he calls them "holy ones" or "saints" (*hagioi* in Greek). This designation is important because early Christians and most Jews believed that those who had lived in obedience to God's will would be raised from the dead on the Last Day. Matthew 27:51–53 thus sends the message that Jesus' death and resurrection were the beginning of the End, the apocalyptic turning point in salvation history.[7]

Paul refers to the risen Jesus as "the firstfruits of those who have fallen asleep" (1 Cor. 15:20 NIV). The imagery of firstfruits implies that Jesus was the only one raised. (Paul writes that Jesus *is* the firstfruits, not that he is *among* the firstfruits.) Paul also teaches that the just will be raised only when Jesus returns to earth. If Paul knew of the event Matthew relates, the logic of his firstfruits metaphor would be ruined. Paul's train of thought shows that he did not know about the event Matthew narrates.

7. Knowing that this is Matthew's meaning helps us make sense of an exceedingly strange feature of the story: though the dead come to life when their tombs are opened at the death of Jesus, they do not leave their tombs until after Jesus leaves his. This makes no sense at all if it is meant to be a report of an actual event. But if the story is

The earthquake is the other feature that conveys Matthew's message. Earthquakes are one of the disasters that prophetic and apocalyptic writings associate with the arrival of the End. These cataclysmic events are used to symbolize the enormous importance and consequences of God's intervention in our history. (We still use this imagery in much the same way today when we speak of an "earthshaking" event. Everyone knows we are not referring to a literal earthquake.) Matthew's mention of an earthquake also helps him explain how the tombs were opened. He uses this symbol again at the scene on Easter morning (28:2), even though he does not need it to explain how Jesus' tomb was opened. As Matthew tells it, an angel rolled away the stone, but Matthew adds the earthquake nonetheless, thereby linking Jesus' resurrection with those in 27:51–53. Jesus' tomb was already empty, so the earthquake is doubly unnecessary here. Its sole function in 28:2 is as an apocalyptic symbol.

Biblical authors intentionally used disasters like earthquakes as symbols. This can be seen clearly in Acts 2, where Luke tells the story of the first Pentecost. People are amazed that they each hear the apostles' preaching in their own language (Acts 2:5–12). Peter explains that what is happening is fulfilling the prophecy of Joel. Peter then quotes a long passage from Joel, part of which reads: "I will show portents in the heaven above and signs on the earth below, blood, and fire, and smoky mist. The sun shall be turned to darkness and the moon to blood, before the coming of the Lord's great and glorious day" (Acts 2:19–20 NRSV, quoting Joel 2:30–31). Note that Peter claims that Joel's prophecy is being fulfilled in the events of Pentecost, not that it will be fulfilled at some future date. Obviously, Peter was not asserting that the moon was literally turning into blood as he spoke, or that the sun was literally being darkened by actual smoke. Peter assumed his audience would understand these apocalyptic descriptions symbolically, and Luke expects his readers to do so as well.

Historians have no real choice but to conclude that the resurrections mentioned in Matthew 27:51–53 did not really happen. Of course, there are some Christians who reason that since everything

---

symbolic, it is fitting that Jesus be the first to leave the abode of the dead—even if Matthew partially compromises Jesus' priority by having others come back to life before him.

in the Bible is historically true, this story must be historically true as well. Laypersons are free to believe anything they want, but historians are not free to claim that something happened simply because they want it to be so—just as juries are not free to reach any verdict they want. Historians and juries must be guided by evidence. And in this case there is no objective evidence for the historicity of the event. Except for those already committed to literalism, very, very few biblical scholars would argue that Matthew 27:51–53 is historical. (It would be interesting to learn Craig's position on this and his reasons for it.)

To sum up, we can reach the same conclusion on the historicity of Matthew 27:51–53 from two directions. On the one hand, we have no objective basis for claiming that the event really happened. On the other hand, we have strong clues from the way Matthew writes the story that he never intended it to be taken literally.

What Did Matthew Think He Was Writing?

If Matthew can create historical fiction like the resurrection of the righteous Jews, what does that mean for the other stories in his Gospel? Perhaps Matthew 27:51–53 is an anomaly, a passage where Matthew proceeds in a way totally unlike the way he writes in the rest of his Gospel. If so, it can tell us nothing about the Evangelists' overall perspective on the kind of truth they intended to communicate. But since there is no good reason to regard Matthew 27:51–53 as an anomaly, we have to assume that it can help us understand Matthew's (and the other Evangelists') perspective on the historical value of the stories in the Gospel.

To gauge how Matthew regarded the historicity of the events he narrates, we have to keep in mind that Matthew relies on Mark as one of his sources. Sometimes he virtually copies from Mark, sometimes he paraphrases. Sometimes he abbreviates Mark's narrative, deleting nonessential details while retaining the substance of the story. At other times, though, Matthew deliberately alters Mark. He does not simply reword the account, but he changes its content in such a way as to alter Mark's meaning—sometimes a little, sometimes a lot; sometimes subtly, sometimes obviously.

An unusually clear example is the way in which Matthew 20:20–23 alters Mark 10:35–40. Mark tells of Jesus teaching his disciples that he will be put to death in Jerusalem (Mark 10:33–34). James and John then approach Jesus with the request that he grant them the places of highest honor when he comes into his glory. Because they had just heard Jesus' prediction of his passion, their request appears incredibly crass and shows that James and John totally failed to grasp the meaning of Jesus' teaching. When Matthew tells this story, he has the mother of James and John make the brazen request on behalf of her sons (Matt. 20:20). Why did Matthew make this change? Did he think that Mark was historically wrong at this point and that he had the real story of what had actually happened? There is not the slightest indication that Matthew made this change to set the record straight. Mark has a number of other scenes in which the disciples act stupidly or selfishly, and each time Matthew alters the scene in such a way that the disciples act wisely and behave as role models for Christians (cf., e.g., the disciples' response to Jesus in Mark 6:51–52 and in Matt. 14:32–33). In the present scene Matthew's small but significant modification enables him to retain the valuable lesson the scene teaches but without besmirching the reputation of the two famous apostles.

There are dozens and dozens of places where Matthew alters Mark. Careful analysis of these changes (a process called redaction criticism) helps us to understand the messages Matthew is communicating through his distinctive version of the words and deeds of Jesus. These changes show beyond the shadow of a doubt that Matthew felt free to change Mark's story when he did not agree with some aspect of its message, or when he believed his changes would make it a better vehicle for his own message. These changes show either that Matthew did not regard Mark's Gospel as a literal report of actual events or that he did not care one way or the other. For Matthew (and, by extrapolation, all the Evangelists), facts were far less important than the meanings they expressed. After all, the facts could be changed to enhance the message.

Turning to the Easter stories, we can see how Matthew has altered Mark's version of the scene at the empty tomb. Two women (not three, as in Mark) go to see the tomb (not to anoint the body) before sunrise (not after). As they arrive, there is an earthquake, during which an angel rolls away the stone, terrifying the guards. (In Mark the women find the stone already rolled away when they arrive; Mark mentions neither an earthquake, nor an angel, nor guards.) Matthew's angel speaks to the women from outside the tomb; in

Mark a young man speaks to them after they step inside. The scene in Matthew concludes when the women, instead of fleeing in fear and telling no one (as in Mark), "depart in fear and great joy" and tell the disciples.

Matthew does not think Mark was misinformed. He is not setting the record straight. It is not a question of whether Matthew is right and Mark is wrong or vice versa. Matthew obviously does not think that Mark gave a literal report of an actual event, and there's no good reason for us to think that Matthew considered his own version to be a literal report either.

Matthew did not write his account to prove that Jesus' resurrection is a fact of history. Did Matthew believe that there was a historical kernel to his story that was literally true—that Jesus had in fact been buried, that people knew where, and that some women had discovered the tomb to be empty? We really don't know, and there is no way of telling from the Gospel he wrote some fifty years after Jesus' death. All we know is that Matthew inherited this story from Mark and felt free to alter it considerably in order to proclaim his faith in Jesus' resurrection. And that, it seems to me, is the key: faith. The Evangelists are interested in faith far more than in facts. We also know that they felt free to invent "facts" by creating stories out of whole cloth if this would enhance their proclamation of faith.

Can Fiction Express Truth?

Our consideration of the story about the earthquake and the rising of the Jewish saints in Matthew 27:51–53 leads to the conclusion that it is not the report of an actual event, that Matthew did not intend it to be, and that his ancient audience understood that. So is the story false? That depends on the precise meaning of the question. If it means, "Is the story a fiction, a narrative of an event that did not in fact happen?" the answer is "Yes, it is false." But if the question means, "Is what the author intends to communicate false?" then we have to ask a more basic question: Is Matthew's message false simply because the story he used to convey it is not historical? Matthew's meaning is that the death and resurrection of Jesus are the turning point in salvation history, God's decisive intervention in human affairs. Are we guilty of what Craig derisively calls Peter Pan theology if we both profess the truth of Matthew's message and acknowledge that Matthew 27:51–53 is not historical?

Well, millions of Christians believe Matthew's message without actually knowing the story of Matthew 27:51–53. (In my long experience as a Bible teacher, many Christians are surprised when they encounter this story. Even those well acquainted with the Bible say things like, "I don't remember reading this before.") This was all the more so in the first century, when very few Christians had access to Matthew's Gospel. Mark, Luke, John, Paul, and the other New Testament authors surely agreed with Matthew that Jesus' death and resurrection were God's decisive act in salvation history, even though nothing indicates that they knew the story related in Matthew 27:51–53.

Another way of getting at the issue is to ask, Which came first, the story or the belief in its message? Does Matthew's story provide the basis for the belief that Jesus' death and resurrection are the decisive event in salvation history, or does the story express this belief? In other words, what caused what? Did the story give rise to the belief, or did the belief give rise to the story? In light of our historical considerations, the answer is clear: the story presumes and expresses the belief in its message. Matthew (or someone in his tradition) created the story to express faith in the supreme spiritual importance of Jesus' death and resurrection. The story is addressed to an audience that believes in Jesus and so understands and believes its message.

Considering the matter from another direction also shows that the story presupposed, rather than gave rise to, faith in Jesus. At the time Matthew wrote his Gospel, Jesus was a very controversial figure. Most Jews rejected the claim that he was the Messiah, a few accepted it (i.e., the Christian Jews, or Jewish Christians—either label will do), but nobody was neutral about Jesus. How could one be? There was no middle ground. It is inconceivable that a serious Jew could have said, "Maybe Jesus is the Messiah, and maybe he isn't; either way is all right with me." Because of the polarized religious situation, Jews who were not followers of Jesus were hostile toward what they thought he stood for and toward his disciples, whose movement posed a threat to Judaism. Now what are the realistic chances that someone like this would read or hear the story in Matthew 27:51–53 and as a result conclude that Jesus must have been the one through whom God had decisively intervened in human history? The odds of that happening are even lower than the odds that any reader will be converted to Islam by reading the Muslim apologetic that I so clumsily outlined above.[8] Matthew's story would simply not persuade outsiders. They would understand its message, but they would reject it on the spot because they would have no prior belief in Jesus. Matthew knew full well that his stories would not persuade Jews hostile to Jesus. In fact, Matthew 28:11–15 explains why many of those who knew Jesus' tomb was empty did not believe in his resurrection.

What Does an Empty Tomb Prove?

Try to see the situation from a Jewish perspective. Matthew 28:11–15 reflects Matthew's bitter animosity toward the Jewish leaders, to whom he here imputes corrupt and deceitful motives. But if we step back from Matthew's extremely one-sided perspective, we realize that all that most Jews knew was that followers of Jesus claimed that he had risen from the dead. To get some idea of how this must have sounded to Jews of the time, imagine our response to reports by some members of a cult that their recently deceased leader (whom they had buried) had risen. Their reports that his grave was empty would hardly persuade many. Even if it was confirmed that the grave where they claim he was buried was empty, what would that prove? Nothing. We would conclude either that they had removed the body or that he was never buried there in the first place. Suppose they told stories of seeing angels at the empty grave or of the grave being opened by an earthquake. Suppose they claimed that our leaders were involved in a conspiracy to cover up the truth about the resurrection of their master. Suppose they told of having seen him alive, of having spoken and eaten with him. And (though I can't imagine how this would come about in our society) suppose that some of these witnesses were willing to die for their belief in their leader.

What would we make of such people and their belief in their messiah? Probably something similar to what ancient people made of the earliest Christians. (As a thought experiment, ask yourself what it would take to convince you that this cult leader had truly risen from the dead.)

---

8. I say "even lower than" rather than "the same as" because the apology at least gives a rational argument whereas Matt. 27:51–53 merely makes an unsupported assertion.

Empty tombs don't prove anything, except to insiders. Nor do reports of appearances of risen leaders. In the Gospels the risen Jesus appears only to those who already believe in him. Those who see him after his resurrection are those who followed him during his lifetime. John's Gospel originally ended with a blessing for those who believe in Jesus without needing to see him firsthand.[9] The implication was that it took little faith to believe when one had actually seen the risen Lord. Matthew, however, does not agree. At the very end of Matthew's Gospel is a fascinating and unexpected statement. He reports that even some of the apostles who saw the risen Jesus in person had their doubts. Just before Jesus sent forth the Eleven with the Great Commission, they prostrated themselves before Jesus, "but some doubted" (Matt. 28:17). This Gospel thus closes with a cryptic admission that even some of these ultimate insiders were not convinced by a face-to-face encounter with the risen Lord. Matthew's abrupt comment comes as a complete surprise, and its precise meaning is puzzling. But this much at least is clear: Whatever else the Gospels may teach about the resurrection, faith in the risen Jesus requires more than stories about him—no matter how convincing these stories may be to some insiders.

9. See John 20:29. The original version of John's Gospel ended at 20:31. Chapter 21 was added in the final edition.

The Jesus of History and the Christ of Faith: Harmony or Conflict?

Craig L. Blomberg

The issues about Jesus that the debate between Crossan and Craig considers are among the most important historically, theologically, and philosophically that could be raised. To have two so lucid and thoughtful representatives of major swaths of contemporary scholarship debating each other in this format is a welcome contribution to the contemporary discussion. I am grateful for the opportunity to give a brief response.

Response to Craig's Opening Address

Dr. Craig begins by correctly identifying two of the most crucial assertions of historic Christianity that are regularly doubted by contemporary critical scholars: the real Jesus rose from the dead and, if not, Christianity is a fairy tale. The second of these assertions, although phrased strongly and perhaps colloquially, is a virtual restatement of Paul's own claim in 1 Corinthians 15:19: "If only for this life we have hope in Christ, we are to be pitied more than all men" (NIV). The first contention is perhaps slightly overstated. Craig writes, "The real Jesus rose from the dead in confirmation of his radical personal claims to divinity" (p. 25). There is implicit Christology throughout the Gospels that points to Jesus' understanding himself as divine, but only rarely is it explicit. Far more common and demonstrable are Jesus' personal claims to messiahship.[1] But for a

Craig L. Blomberg is professor of New Testament at Denver Seminary.

1. This is a major thesis of several recent works, most notably Ben Witherington III, *The Christology of Jesus* (Minneapolis: Fortress, 1990); John P. Meier, *A Marginal Jew*, 3 vols. (New York: Doubleday, 1991–); Peter Stuhlmacher, *Jesus of Nazareth—Christ of Faith* (Peabody, Mass.: Hendrickson, 1993); Markus Bockmuehl, *This Jesus: Martyr, Lord, Messiah* (Edinburgh: T. and T. Clark, 1994); N. T.

first-century Jew, to be a messiah did not necessarily mean to be divine.[2] I believe both claims emerge from the text of the Gospels, but the two are not identical. When Craig goes on to quote the German theologian Pöhlmann that there is "virtually a consensus . . . that Jesus came on the scene with *an unheard-of authority*, namely, the authority of God" (p. 25), Pöhlmann is clearly not speaking of a consensus that Jesus claimed outright to be deity, the Second Person of the Trinity. Such a virtual consensus does not exist by any stretch of the imagination. But this caveat does not vitiate Craig's main point. The resurrection must be understood as a vindication of Jesus' prior claims for his person and ministry, as Tom Wright has so cogently reminded us in his recent magisterial *Jesus and the Victory of God*.[3]

Craig proceeds to support his first contention with what he calls four highly significant facts. Each of these facts is a crucial component in developing any case for the historical credibility of the resurrection. Each point seems well taken, and their cumulative force should not be missed. Nevertheless, a few qualifying remarks are in order.

Regarding Fact (1), it might have been good if Craig had simply referred to the historicity of Jesus' burial in a tomb that could easily have been identified. To tie this largely uncontroverted contention to Joseph of Arimathea makes the point at least slightly more suspect historically. Again, there is overstatement in Craig's comment that "the vast majority of New Testament critics concur that Jesus was buried by Joseph of Arimathea in his own tomb." Raymond Brown's thorough study of the passion narratives demonstrates the diversity of scholarly discussion at this point, even though a good case for the historicity of the Joseph material can still be made.[4] Once again, Craig

---

Wright, *Jesus and the Victory of God* (Minneapolis: Fortress, 1996). Even more widespread is the belief that Jesus saw himself as God's final eschatological agent, which is defined in a variety of ways, not always in terms of messiahship. A thorough review of the current state of the question is found in Ben Witherington III, *The Jesus Quest* (Downers Grove, Ill.: InterVarsity, 1995).

2. For a survey of the diversity of first-century Jewish messianic hope, see James H. Charlesworth, ed., *The Messiah: Developments in Earliest Judaism and Christianity* (Minneapolis: Fortress, 1992).

3. See n. 1.

4. Raymond E. Brown, *The Death of the Messiah,* 2 vols. (Garden City, N.Y.: Doubleday, 1994), 2:1205–41. A recent example of scholarly skepticism appears in Gerald O'Collins and Daniel Kendall, "Did Joseph of Arimathea Exist?" *Biblica* 75 (1994): 235–41.

appeals to a supporting quotation from another scholar (J. A. T. Robinson) who makes precisely the less sweeping kind of statement that might have been good for Craig himself to make: "The burial of Jesus is one of the most certain facts about the historical Jesus" (p. 27).

The same pattern of slight overstatement followed by a supporting quotation that makes the point more cautiously recurs with Fact (2). It is unquestionably true, as Kremer states, that "most scholars hold firmly to the reliability of the biblical statements concerning the empty tomb" (p. 27). Whether most scholars would agree that the tomb was first found empty on the Sunday following the crucifixion, and that the discovery was first made by a group of women followers, is slightly more questionable. Still, there are two points in this stronger statement that merit further unpacking. As Craig himself notes in one of his subpoints, "the fact that women's testimony was considered worthless in first-century Palestine" makes it highly unlikely that early Christians would have invented a story with women as the first witnesses of the resurrection (p. 27). Second, as Craig stresses in many other writings, something must have happened on that precise Sunday to lead a group of Jewish disciples to begin gathering for worship not on the Sabbath, the Jewish holy day of rest, but on the first day of the week, despite the difficulties which that created in an era when Sunday was not yet a day off work.[5]

Fact (3) together with the exposition following is the most accurately stated thus far, but it is also the least significant apologetically. It is indeed "almost universally acknowledged by New Testament scholars today" that various individuals and groups believed they had some kind of genuine experience of the risen Jesus (p. 28). But was that experience a vision? a hallucination? a mystical communion with God? a subjective impression? or a genuine objective event to which any witnesses present could have testified? As it is stated, Fact (3) does not allow us to claim that the last of these options is the most reasonable, yet that is precisely what classic Christianity has believed.

5. For a concise elaboration of these and related arguments by Craig himself, see his "Did Jesus Rise from the Dead?" in *Jesus under Fire*, ed. Michael J. Wilkins and J. P. Moreland (Grand Rapids: Zondervan, 1995), 141–76. For comprehensive detail see his two books, *The Historical Argument for the Resurrection of Jesus* (Lewiston, N.Y.: Edwin Mellen, 1985); and *Assessing the New Testament Evidence for the Historicity of the Resurrection of Jesus* (Lewiston, N.Y.: Edwin Mellen, 1989).

Fact (4) may be the strongest of all. Subpoints (b) and (c) are particularly telling. The crucifixion should have disproved any previous claims made by Jesus or beliefs that his disciples had about him. By the criterion of Deuteronomy 21:23, he was accursed by God. And if the disciples were hallucinating, there was nothing in their experience to lead them to imagine a Jesus risen from the dead prior to the general resurrection of all God's people at the end of the world. This latter point is particularly worth stressing because of Gerd Lüdemann's revival of the hallucination hypothesis and the Jesus Seminar's general approval of it.[6] The only qualifying remark that Craig's first subpoint (a) merits is that most conservative Christians insist that there is evidence that at least a minority strand of pre-Christian Judaism interpreted Isaiah 52–53 in a messianic way; there is, then, at least some slight precedent for belief in a dying Messiah.[7]

As Craig turns to Crossan's work, he cites four counterclaims to the four points he has just made. Craig then proceeds to identify four presuppositions which he believes have led to Crossan's denials of the four facts. These presuppositions involve the supposed reliability of parts of the Gospel of Peter and the so-called Secret Gospel of Mark, the attribution of substantial creativity to the early church with respect to the Jesus tradition, and an antisupernaturalist worldview. Craig's objections are well taken. The first two of the four presuppositions are particularly idiosyncratic,[8] although the latter two are widely held. Nevertheless, the extent to which the Jesus Seminar has accepted all four of these presuppositions[9] makes Craig's case again somewhat overstated when, for example, he says that "no major New Testament scholar agrees with [Crossan's] view" (p. 30). Not least because of his voluminous publishing and frequent media

6. Gerd Lüdemann, *The Resurrection of Jesus: History, Experience, Theology* (Minneapolis: Fortress, 1994); idem, *What Really Happened to Jesus?* (Louisville: Westminster John Knox, 1995). Lüdemann uses the terms *vision* and *hallucination* interchangeably (see, e.g., *What Really Happened?* 99, 100). Whereas "vision" for most writers suggests the possibility of an external, albeit immaterial, origin of a phenomenon, Lüdemann makes it clear he is referring strictly to a human subject's inward psychological creation (pp. 117–18).

7. See, classically, Joachim Jeremias, "*Pais Theou* in Later Judaism in the Period after the LXX," in *Theological Dictionary of the New Testament*, ed. Gerhard Kittel and Gerhard Friedrich, 10 vols. (Grand Rapids: Eerdmans, 1964–76), 5:677–700.

8. Contrast Meier, *Marginal Jew*, 1:112–66.

9. Robert W. Funk with Mahlon H. Smith, *The Gospel of Mark: Red-Letter Edition* (Sonoma, Calif.: Polebridge, 1991), 1–26.

appearances, Crossan's perspectives have influenced not only the Jesus Seminar, but a considerable scattering of unpublished or little-known university professors in departments of religious studies around the country.

The end of Craig's opening address finally brings him to his second contention that the rationality of Christianity rises or falls with the resurrection. It is a pity that the constraints of time did not permit him to elaborate on this point at all. Clearly, there is a large swath of Christian scholarship based on a fideistic, rather than an evidentialist, apologetic. Numerous sincere churchgoers profess, and perhaps recite weekly in liturgical creeds, far more theology than they believe can be demonstrated on historical grounds. From a philosopher's point of view, one may wish to dub this kind of faith irrational, perhaps even schizophrenic, but the position requires a considerably more nuanced response than to refer to Peter Pan.[10]

As one who has read and appreciated many of Craig's published works, I know that he has said elsewhere much that I have pointed out. It is too bad that the format of the debate allowed both participants so little time for their opening addresses, for I am sure that Craig would have filled in many of the apparent gaps had he been given the time. And although Craig may in some instances overstate his points, his two major contentions and primary supporting arguments do indeed seem to take the discussion in the direction in which it needs to go.

Response to Crossan's Opening Address

Crossan's material is simpler and attempts to cover less ground. Therefore, critique at this point can proceed more quickly. By distinguishing between the real Jesus and the historical Jesus, Crossan raises the very issue I noted above. Scholars often believe much more about Jesus than they think can be defended historically. This is an important distinction and one that is not always clear in massive tomes dealing with the historical Jesus.[11] On the other hand, there

10. I would argue that there are room and necessity for both a fideist and an evidentialist apologetic, as put forward in Ronald B. Mayers, *Both/And: A Balanced Apologetic* (Chicago: Moody, 1984).
11. Not least of which is Crossan's own *The Historical Jesus* (San Francisco: Harper, 1991).

are plenty of critics who will not believe anything beyond that which can be demonstrated on historical grounds.

As for Crossan's first presupposition, his presumption of Markan priority, this, too, is reasonable. While not inviolable, it is a tenet of scholarship held so widely across all the major theological traditions as to be inherently probable. Crossan's second presupposition—that there are three successive layers of Gospel material involving Jesus' words and deeds—is also potentially unobjectionable. Indeed, in one form it seems to be demanded by Luke 1:1–4. In this, the most explicit of the Gospel writers' statements as to how they composed their documents, Luke refers to the very three stages Crossan and most other scholars identify. There is information that was retold by "eyewitnesses and servants of the word" (v. 2b). This in turn was "handed down" in the oral tradition (v. 2a). The Greek verb here is almost a technical one for this kind of transmission. Third, initial written documents were compiled on the basis of the two previous stages: "Many have undertaken to draw up an account of the things that have been fulfilled among us" (v. 1). Luke numbers himself among the "many": "It seemed good also to me to write an orderly account . . . so that you may know the certainty of the things you have been taught" (vv. 3–4 NIV). In short, Luke has his own ideological or theological purposes, potentially distinct from the purposes of others who preceded him.[12]

Where Crossan and conservatives differ comes with his comments about how the Gospels "update the story" (p. 34). He does not elaborate on these remarks, but his writings elsewhere, like those of many scholars of our day, make it obvious that a degree of creativity which the evidence does not demand is being attributed to the Gospel tradition.[13] A careful comparison of the Synoptics makes it abundantly clear that the Evangelists selected what they believed was relevant for the particular Christian communities that they were addressing. The differences between parallel accounts demonstrate that selection, paraphrase, abbreviation, interpretation, and abstraction all took

12. For a book-length evangelical study making precisely these points, see Robert H. Stein, *The Synoptic Problem* (Grand Rapids: Baker, 1987).

13. Besides his *Historical Jesus,* see especially John Dominic Crossan, *In Parables: The Challenge of the Historical Jesus* (New York: Harper and Row, 1973); idem, *In Fragments: The Aphorisms of Jesus* (San Francisco: Harper and Row, 1983); and idem, *Who Killed Jesus?* (San Francisco: Harper, 1995).

place, all fully within the historiographical conventions of the day. But none of this variation requires us to conclude that the Evangelists distorted, falsified, or invented history at any point.[14] To the extent that this more drastic type of creativity forms part of Crossan's presuppositional pool, he should investigate whether an evenhanded dealing with the evidence in fact demands it.

The bulk of Crossan's opening address gets to the real heart of the debate between many evangelicals and many liberals. What genre are the Gospels? What genre are those stories in the Gospels that contain apparently miraculous elements? Even more specifically, what genre are the stories with which the Gospel accounts typically begin and end—namely, the accounts of the virginal conception in Matthew and Luke and the stories of the resurrection in all four Gospels? Here are the really crucial questions which we should be debating at greater length.

On the one hand, there is no methodological reason to object to Crossan's approach at this point. If, in fact, a plausible case can be made that the closest generic parallels to various parts of the Gospels, or to the Gospels in their entirety, are mythological (legendary, parabolic, etc.), then that is how they should be interpreted. Clearly, parable, legend, and myth can all reveal theological truths, as at least parables do consistently for Jesus within the pages of the Gospels.[15] But the key question is whether, in fact, this is the correct identification of genre.

Appeal to the creation narratives is not very helpful. I actually think a better case can be made for a nonliteral interpretation of Genesis 1 than Crossan has suggested here.[16] Such an interpretation would be consistent with the views known alternately as progressive creation or theistic evolution. These views posit that the creative acts of God correspond broadly to the major stages in evolutionary theory, though not entirely in sequence. They also stress that the details

14. See Craig L. Blomberg, *The Historical Reliability of the Gospels* (Downers Grove, Ill.: InterVarsity, 1987); and idem, "Where Do We Start Studying Jesus?" in *Jesus under Fire*, ed. Wilkins and Moreland, 18–50; and the wealth of literature cited in both studies.

15. See Craig L. Blomberg, *Interpreting the Parables* (Downers Grove, Ill.: InterVarsity, 1990).

16. See Henri Blocher, *In the Beginning* (Downers Grove, Ill.: InterVarsity, 1984), with Conrad Hyers, *The Meaning of Creation* (Atlanta: John Knox, 1984).

of scientific evolution at the macrolevel are far less secure than evidence for microlevel evolution within species.[17]

On the other hand, I remain unconvinced that the closest parallels to the accounts of Jesus' virginal conception and other miraculous elements of the Gospels are found in pagan mythology. With respect to the virgin birth, J. Gresham Machen disproved this theory with copious evidence more than sixty years ago, and he has not been refuted.[18] And a wide cross-section of contemporary interpretation of the miracles generally acknowledges parallels in Judaism and in the Old Testament to be more telling than parallels in the myths of the ancient Greco-Roman world.[19] A careful reading of the patristic evidence suggests that indeed the vast majority of early Christians did believe that the type of information the Gospel writers communicated was historical fact, even as they recognized the more superficial parallels with the mythology of other worldviews.[20] The idea that the Gospel miracle stories were intended to be viewed as myths is itself largely the product of the so-called scientific Enlightenment of the last two hundred years.

Response to Craig's Rebuttal

I shall confine myself at this point to six discrete remarks:

1. Clearly, both initial addresses dealt largely with different issues and hence talked past each other. Craig is right to point out that Crossan did not address, much less refute, most of what Craig initially said. Had the two gone in reverse order with the identical addresses, a similar observation could have been made of Craig's comments vis-à-vis Crossan's.

2. Unlike Craig, I do not understand Crossan's distinction between the real Jesus and the historical Jesus to be equivalent to the dichotomy between metaphorical and literal interpretations. Rather,

17. See especially Phillip E. Johnson, *Darwin on Trial* (Downers Grove, Ill.: Inter-Varsity, 1991).

18. J. Gresham Machen, *The Virgin Birth of Christ* (New York: Harper, 1930).

19. David Wenham and Craig L. Blomberg, eds., *Gospel Perspectives* (Sheffield: JSOT, 1986), vol. 6, and the literature there cited. On the historical authenticity of the miracles in the Gospels as gauged by the standard criteria, see Meier, *Marginal Jew*, 2:509–1038.

20. Harold Remus, *Pagan-Christian Conflict over Miracle in the Second Century* (Cambridge, Mass.: Philadelphia Patristic Foundation, 1983).

Crossan seems to distinguish between, on the one hand, what the literal Jesus actually did and said and, on the other, what he did and said that can be demonstrated by historical study.

3. I am also not at all clear that the statement "Dr. Crossan knows that the Gospels are not of the genre of myth or allegory or folk story or fairy tale" (p. 41) is true. It would seem that one or more of those genres is precisely what Crossan is identifying the Gospels as, at least in part if not in toto. But Craig is right to pursue the question of genre. And he correctly identifies Hemer's as the outstanding study with respect to the Book of Acts. Not quite as detailed but also very much worth mentioning as bolstering Craig's case with respect to the Gospels are Richard Burridge's studies on the genres of Matthew, Mark, Luke, and John.[21]

4. Craig's response to the alleged parallels to the story of the virginal conception is again moving the discussion in the right direction. And, as we suggested above, given greater time and space, the argument could be strengthened. The Gospel narratives of Jesus' conception are remarkably brief and unadorned—in striking contrast to all of the so-called parallels in both the Greco-Roman world and in Judaism; and almost nothing is made of the doctrine of the virgin birth in the rest of the New Testament. If this were indeed a case of later Christian theologizing in mythical garb, we would expect the doctrine to play a much more important role in the Epistles and indeed in the rest of the theology of the Evangelists themselves.[22]

5. Craig is correct also to pursue the issue of the resurrection. The argument that this belief arose first of all in Jewish circles, rather than in the larger Hellenistic world, is a strong one that needs to be pressed. Had Jesus lived and ministered in Athens, and had his message spread to Israel a generation or two later, the subjective-vision hypothesis would be plausible. One could imagine that stories which originally attributed to Jesus nothing more than the immortality of his soul had become objectified in a Jewish environment that be-

21. Richard A. Burridge, *What Are the Gospels? A Comparison with Graeco-Roman Biography* (Cambridge: Cambridge University Press, 1992); this volume has in part been popularized under the title *Four Gospels, One Jesus?* (Grand Rapids: Eerdmans, 1994).

22. For recent defenses of the historicity of the virginal conception, see C. E. B. Cranfield, "Some Reflections on the Subject of the Virgin Birth," *Scottish Journal of Theology* 41 (1988): 177–89; H. Douglas Buckwalter, "The Virgin Birth of Jesus Christ: A Union of Theology and History," *Evangelical Journal* 13 (1995): 3–14.

lieved strongly in a corporeal resurrection. But given the fact that the direction of development of Christian proclamation and doctrine was precisely the reverse, from a first generation of thoroughly Jewish Christians to later widespread impact in the Hellenistic world, it is implausible that the original story within Christianity would have involved anything less than an affirmation of the objective, physical reawakening of Christ's body from the grave.

6. I also agree that Crossan's pure fideism leaves him with no rational reason to worship the historic Christian Jesus, though we must be glad that he still does. One may not have any reason for believing that a car will run, and yet on the basis of sheer faith get in it, start it, and discover that, in fact, it takes one to one's destination. So Craig's final paragraph (p. 44) seems to be slightly overstated. One can hope that things are true, even when one is not convinced there is enough historical evidence to prove them; one can then act upon those hopes, and be pleasantly surprised to find that in fact they turn out to be true and do what they promise. But the point is also well taken that such an epistemological foundation is a shaky one indeed. Without a stronger evidentialist basis for faith, one's Christian commitment often rests on little more than an accident of history and the place of one's birth. Had one not been raised in a Christian environment, it is doubtful if a person without stronger reasons for believing would have ever come to Christian faith.

Responses to Crossan's Rebuttal

Again I shall simply list my points of critique seriatim:

1. Crossan's delineation of his view as an intermediate position between historic supernaturalism and full-fledged naturalism is a helpful one, particularly because it is not clearly present in his major work, *The Historical Jesus*. In light of this delineation it is inappropriate for Craig to call Crossan's position full-fledged naturalism, but that does not make Crossan right. Crossan actually advances no arguments for his views here, but merely clarifies what they are.

2. Crossan takes Craig to task in the same way that I did earlier with respect to his appeal to a majority of scholars, as well as with respect to Craig's phrasing concerning Jesus' claims to be God. In the process, Crossan himself seems to engage in at least slight overstatement when attributing to Craig the view that "a majority of New Testament scholars say that Jesus claimed he was God" (p. 46). That

is not exactly what Craig said, although his language leaves itself open to that misinterpretation.

3. The argument from Paul's use of the metaphor of firstfruits for the resurrection to the view that the entire resurrection accounts are metaphorical is a slippery one indeed. The conclusion by no means logically follows. It is one thing for a writer to use metaphor or analogy to explain a wholly unparalleled form of existence (resurrection life); it is an entirely different point to claim that such existence is itself metaphorical and not literal. Crossan still has not rebutted any of Craig's major arguments for interpreting the resurrection accounts as stories of a literal bodily reawakening to life, nor refuted any of the arguments for their historicity.

4. Crossan needs to read Craig's elaboration elsewhere of what Paul means by "spiritual body" in 1 Corinthians 15.[23] As Craig also clarifies later in the debate (pp. 51–52), "spiritual" here means "supernatural" as opposed to natural or mortal; it does not mean noncorporeal. Crossan's description of what a dockworker at Corinth might have imagined upon hearing Paul speak about the resurrection might reflect misconceptions that could have arisen in the Greco-Roman world. But Crossan's perspective is not easily imaginable in the Jewish world, where resurrection faith first emerged. So again, the key point to be pressed here is that Paul's faith, like early Christian faith in the resurrection more generally, emerged in a Jewish milieu and remained couched in thoroughly Jewish terminology.

5. At the end of Crossan's rebuttal we come back to the heart of the fideist-evidentialist debate. And now it is Crossan's turn to engage in drastic overstatement: "We never believe in anything else [i.e., other than metaphor]. We don't need faith for facts" (p. 47). My response is, "Sometimes yes, sometimes no." Neither writer has commented on the uniqueness of Christianity (along with Judaism and Islam) in demanding historical events at its core; this sharply contrasts with the Greco-Roman and Eastern religions, which Crossan has cited with respect to divine births.[24]

23. See William Lane Craig, "The Bodily Resurrection of Jesus," in *Gospel Perspectives,* ed. R. T. France and David Wenham (1980), 1:47–74. See also Gordon D. Fee, *The First Epistle to the Corinthians* (Grand Rapids: Eerdmans, 1987), 775–86; Craig L. Blomberg, *1 Corinthians* (Grand Rapids: Zondervan, 1994), 315–16.

24. See Norman Anderson, *Christianity and World Religions: The Challenge of Pluralism* (Downers Grove, Ill.: InterVarsity, 1984); idem, ed., *The World's Religions,* 4th ed. (Grand Rapids: Eerdmans, 1975).

Response to the Dialogue

Trying to evaluate the dialogue itself is particularly frustrating because it seems that none of the speakers is getting at the heart of the issue. Craig is correct to raise the question of God's existence in the Jurassic age, and Crossan's reply that this is a meaningless question itself makes no sense. There clearly is an issue of objectivity here that he is not addressing. On the other hand, Crossan does seem right to stress that Christianity requires faith. It's not clear if Craig is arguing that God's existence or the resurrection or the historical Jesus can be so objectively and factually delineated that no leap of faith ever enters in.

It is good that Craig gets a chance here to clarify the distinction between pre- and postresurrection bodies, although it's too bad that the discussion gets sidetracked to the idea that a preresurrection body is necessarily sinful. Crossan again confuses matters by not distinguishing between resurrection talk per se and metaphors that are used to illustrate the resurrection.

When the discussion turns to the passion narratives, things become remarkably topsy-turvy. Crossan's remarks seem misleading. In his other writings, especially *Who Killed Jesus?* he is quite adamant that, except for the barest of detail, the passion narratives were invented on the basis of Old Testament texts. But here he seems to be contrasting the objectivity and historicity of the passion narratives with the diversity of geographical perspective and other detail in the resurrection narratives. Either the passion narratives are, as Crossan declares elsewhere, among the least historical parts of the Gospels, or they are much more solidly grounded, as Crossan here claims. One cannot have it both ways.

The fact is, even those who accept the historicity and objectivity of the passion narratives, which start with Jesus' traveling to Jerusalem, admit that there is every bit as much diversity in them as in the resurrection narratives. Did Jesus follow an apparently short, straight-line itinerary from Galilee to Judea, as Matthew 19 and Mark 10 seem to suggest? Or was there a lengthy period of a so-called Perean ministry or at least of itinerant travel, as Luke 9:51–18:34 implies? Or did Jesus go back and forth to Jerusalem, staying in the environs of the city for several months before his crucifixion, as John 7–11 might lead one to believe? And, of course, the apparent discrepancies in more minor details, as well as the distinctive theologies of the four Evangelists, are every bit as obvious in the passion narratives as in the resurrection accounts.[25]

None of this detail nor its diversity, wherever found, necessarily calls into question the historicity of the accounts. Plausible harmonizations have been suggested;[26] indeed, a cautious form of harmonization is a foundational method among all classicists and historians of antiquity. What is more, once the theological perspectives, including those conveyed by where each Evangelist locates Jesus geographically while en route to Jerusalem, are understood, then the reasons for the apparent discrepancies often become evident, and the plausibility of the harmonizations is enhanced.[27] At most, the resurrection narratives are only slightly more diverse than any other major parallel accounts in the Gospels. And this diversity is understandable because the resurrection formed the central theological affirmation of early Christianity; here, if anywhere, the Evangelists wished to bring out the depth and richness of the material treated. Crossan simply evades the issue of plausible harmonizations that Craig rightly brings up. In fact, the wealth of detailed, nuanced evangelical scholarship that writers of Crossan's bent simply ignore altogether is astonishing.[28] Even more audaciously, Crossan elsewhere declares, "In quoting *secondary* literature I spend no time citing other scholars to show how wrong they are."[29] An evangelical writer attempting this approach would be laughed out of court; by what criterion does Crossan even deserve a hearing?[30]

25. See Brown, *Death of the Messiah*, for comprehensive detail.

26. See any of the commentaries on the individual Gospels in such series as the Word Biblical Commentary, New International Commentary on the New Testament, Baker Exegetical Commentary on the New Testament, Expositor's Bible Commentary, New American Commentary, Tyndale New Testament Commentary, New International Greek Testament Commentary, and Eerdmans' Pillar volumes.

27. Craig L. Blomberg, "The Legitimacy and Limits of Harmonization," in *Hermeneutics, Authority, and Canon*, ed. D. A. Carson and John D. Woodbridge (Grand Rapids: Zondervan, 1986; Grand Rapids: Baker, 1995 reprint), 135–74.

28. In Crossan's *Historical Jesus*, out of approximately 350 entries in the bibliography I could identify only 3 written by avowed evangelicals. And all of these were historical rather than theological studies.

29. Ibid., xxxiv.

30. Note, too, that the impetus for the present volume came from evangelicals sponsoring a debate, an evangelical editor, and an evangelical publishing house. Where are the comparable works emerging from mainline Protestant or Catholic publishers or major university presses?

Another point at which the discussion gets particularly confused is when Crossan questions Buckley's claims as to what is corroborated by a majority of scholars (p. 54). But instead of pursuing that legitimate line of reasoning, he abandons it, accepts (wrongly) that he reflects a tiny minority, and then winds up finding virtue in being on the side of the few. In matter of fact, Craig's position is probably the minority view, but if that were made clear, then presumably Crossan wouldn't want to push his line of argumentation about God's favoring minorities!

The follow-up dialogue proceeds to broader epistemological questions but without any satisfactory resolution of them. One disclosure by Crossan, however, proves particularly significant. He notes that it was not an epistemological process that led him to belief in God: "I think that it was probably that I grew up with it as part of the very fabric of my being. I've never seen any reason to challenge it. I've never seen any argument persuading me against it. But I don't think I really argued myself into it by logic" (p. 58). Doubtless the same could be said by many conservative Christians, but in neither case are we left with any rational apologetic for faith. People are Christians because they were raised in that tradition and have never successfully detached themselves from it, even though in Crossan's case he has redefined key elements. But that apparently is his only justification for being where he is and what he is.

As the discussion turns to the Johannine emphasis on signs, Crossan pays attention to only one-half of that emphasis. On the one hand, John is skeptical of a faith based merely on signs. In John 2:23–25 many believe in Jesus because of his miracles, but he does not trust that such faith is adequate. In 4:48 Jesus laments, "Unless you people see miraculous signs and wonders . . . , you will not believe." And in his famous reply to Thomas's profession of faith in 20:29, Jesus declares, "Because you have seen me, you have believed; blessed are those who have not seen and yet have believed." On the other hand, in the purpose statement for the entire Gospel in the very next two verses, the fourth Evangelist goes on to write, "Jesus did many other miraculous signs in the presence of his disciples, which are not recorded in this book. But these are written that you may believe that Jesus is the Christ, the Son of God, and that by believing you may have life in his name" (NIV). And going back to the beginning of John's Gospel, we see evidence for this motif as well. John characterizes each of the first two signs of Jesus as a stimulus to belief (2:11; 4:53–54).[31] This, I think, is a stronger rebuttal to Crossan's one-sided appropriation of Johannine theology than to try to argue, as Craig does, for belief on the basis of apostolic testimony and tradition, a position which, as Crossan points out, is not explicit in the text (though still arguable).

The next section of the dialogue raises the important distinction between, on the one hand, those who experience mere visions and narrate them in imagery already conceivable to them, and, on the other, those who have more historically objective experiences of the supernatural and often introduce new concepts previously not conceived. Craig does well to press Crossan on this issue; but again, conversation does not reach satisfactory resolution before Buckley changes the topic, and the issue remains unresolved even when they do get back to it later. The dialogue closes with equally frustrating exchanges that accomplish little. Crossan either does not grasp the force of Craig's arguments based on the early dating of the resurrection traditions, or chooses to ignore it. And Buckley overshoots the mark with his statement about Crossan's logic enabling one to prove that Lincoln killed Booth rather than vice versa.

A Response to the Three Closing Statements

Craig offers a clear and succinct summary, not only of the points he has tried to make, but also of Crossan's failure to address them and of the unconvincingness of Crossan's views. Crossan, on the other hand, does not attempt to summarize his case or the results of the conversation, but he merely explains his rationale for participating in this kind of debate and expresses his hope that similar dialogue might continue. Perhaps the truest and most poignant statement he makes is, "But the ultimate ecumenism will be when liberal Christians talk to conservative Christians" (p. 71). And that, in fact, is the right way to phrase it. With a handful of exceptions, conservative Christians have been trying ever since their resurgence in the scholarly world after World War II to engage liberal Christian scholarship in arguments that take their viewpoints into account. But rather than

31. See, e.g., Robert Kysar, *John, the Maverick Gospel* (Atlanta: John Knox, 1976), 67–73.

being engaged, they've largely been ignored. At least Crossan was willing to talk in the same forum and on the same platform with Craig, even if, unfortunately, a substantial portion of his remarks continued to ignore the actual arguments that Craig put forward. When forums of this nature do indeed engage the most cogent arguments of each side in an evenhanded give-and-take, then true progress will have been made.

Buckley's closing comments begin with remarks of a rather general nature. He offers a succinct and relatively accurate summary of Crossan's and Craig's views and a closing appeal which ends with a sentence that reflects the possible results of a detailed and compelling apologetic for the existence of God and the resurrection of Jesus: "It is much easier to assume (is it not?) that there is a divine transcendent order that has given to our lives what keenness they have and inspired our idealism, and that the risen Christ is the source of that special Christian idealism which brings us together" (p. 73). Unfortunately, Craig has not had the time to expand on his arguments to make this conclusion follow as it should, and Crossan, for the most part, has not had the consideration to engage those arguments. Thus, within the constraints of this forum, it is not clear that either speaker has succeeded in making an ultimately persuasive case for his position or against the alternatives. Perhaps future forums will adopt a format that will allow the more detailed argumentation to continue. Meanwhile, we can be grateful to both scholars for having whetted our appetites for a main course which has yet to be served.

The attempt to distinguish between the Jesus of history and the Christ of faith is a legitimate enterprise. One cannot give historical evidence to support all of the details about the person and work of Jesus recorded in the canonical Gospels. Nevertheless, the historical evidence that is available supports the presumption of at least the general trustworthiness of particularly the Synoptic tradition.[32] When sources repeatedly prove trustworthy where they can be tested, they should be given the benefit of the doubt where they cannot.[33] This is what is frequently referred to as placing the burden of

32. See Blomberg, *Historical Reliability*; Witherington, *Christology*; and Wright, *Jesus and the Victory of God.*

33. I. Howard Marshall, *Luke: Historian and Theologian,* 3d ed. (Exeter: Paternoster, 1988), 21–76.

proof on the skeptic when it comes to Gospel historicity.[34] Kierkegaard is quite correct in saying that there is ultimately a leap of faith that goes beyond what historical evidence can demonstrate. But contra Kierkegaard, it is not an absurd leap. One may liken the situation to a long jumper who runs as far as she can down the track but ultimately must leap into the pit beyond the track. The situation that many skeptics would have us imagine is that the long jumper actually begins running away from the pit, somehow has to pivot and reverse direction, and then jump in the direction of the pit. Such a faith would indeed be irrational and absurd, but that is not the situation we actually face. Historical evidence moves us a long way towards demonstrating our belief; as a result, the faith that is necessary to fill in the remaining gap is reasonable.

A proper historiography must allow for the miraculous as a possible explanation for events that cannot be plausibly explained otherwise.[35] The only way to avoid this conclusion is to begin with an antisupernaturalist or atheist bias. If there is a God similar to the one theists postulate, then it is eminently reasonable that at times of his choosing he should wish to intervene in the space-time universe and generate events not otherwise attributable to natural processes. Conservative Christian believers have sometimes laid themselves open to charges of inconsistency when they are unprepared to consider the miraculous as a legitimate explanation for nonbiblical events. But it may well be that genuine miracles have occurred at Lourdes and elsewhere.[36] Nor is God the only supernatural power in the cosmos able to create a miracle. Contemporary testimonies of demon possessions and exorcisms remind us of a much more malignant supernatural power.[37]

It is also well to keep in view that allowing for the miraculous is not inherently unscientific. John Meier's massive and painstaking

---

34. Stewart C. Goetz and Craig L. Blomberg, "The Burden of Proof," *Journal for the Study of the New Testament* 11 (1981): 39–63.

35. See *In Defense of Miracles: A Comprehensive Case for God's Action in History*, ed. R. Douglas Geivett and Gary R. Habermas (Downers Grove, Ill.: InterVarsity, 1997).

36. Leopold Sabourin, *The Divine Miracles Discussed and Defended* (Rome: Catholic Book Agency, 1977), 152–64.

37. See, e.g., John Richards, *But Deliver Us from Evil* (London: Darton, Longman and Todd, 1974); John W. Montgomery, ed., *Demon Possession* (Minneapolis: Bethany Fellowship, 1976); Anthony N. S. Lane, ed., *The Unseen World: Christian Reflections on Angels, Demons and the Heavenly Realm* (Grand Rapids: Baker, 1996).

study of the historical Jesus documents a large number of "modern scientific people" who nevertheless believe in the possibility of the miraculous, a fact with which Bultmann apparently failed to reckon.[38] Nor will it do to accuse all ancient people of the gullibility characteristic of a prescientific age. Lucian of Samosata, among others, was quick to distinguish between genuine and counterfeit miracles, even in the New Testament world.[39] The highly influential philosophical skepticism of David Hume and its Christian mutation, well described by Van Harvey, in which supernatural explanations by definition remain outside the domain of the historian,[40] is methodologically and philosophically untenable.[41] Reminding us that a growing number of scholars agree, Craig Evans has shown how the standard criteria of historicity can be applied to apparently miraculous events in both ancient and modern sources.[42] One must simply assess each claim on a case-by-case basis.

In short, Craig's reconstruction proves far superior to Crossan's in terms of fitting the facts of the early history of first-century Christianity. More detailed elaboration is certainly needed, given the constraints of time and space in this debate. But such elaboration is readily available. The inability of all of the alternative hypotheses, ancient and modern, to explain away the empty tomb, the resurrection appearances, and the rise of the Christian faith from an utterly defeated band of Jesus' followers, leads us back to an unquestionably supernatural explanation, namely, the true bodily resurrection of Jesus of Nazareth.[43]

38. Meier, *Marginal Jew*, 2:509–34.

39. See his *The Lover of Lies, or the Doubter (Philopseudes sive incredulus)*.

40. Van A. Harvey, *The Historian and the Believer* (New York: Macmillan, 1966).

41. See, respectively, René Latourelle, *The Miracles of Jesus and the Theology of Miracles* (New York: Paulist, 1988); and Colin Brown, *Miracles and the Critical Mind* (Grand Rapids: Eerdmans, 1984).

42. Craig A. Evans, "Life-of-Jesus Research and the Eclipse of Mythology," *Theological Studies* 54 (1993): 3–36.

43. For elaboration on this perspective and on many related points in this debate, see George E. Ladd, *I Believe in the Resurrection of Jesus* (Grand Rapids: Eerdmans, 1975); Murray J. Harris, *From Grave to Glory* (Grand Rapids: Zondervan, 1990); Stephen T. Davis, *Risen Indeed* (Grand Rapids: Eerdmans, 1993); and Gary R. Habermas, *The Resurrection of Jesus* (Grand Rapids: Baker, 1980).

The Irrelevancy of the Empty Tomb

Marcus Borg

I wish to thank Paul Copan, the editor of this volume, for the invitation to take part in this discussion of the meaning and significance of the resurrection of Jesus. I do so as both a scholar and a committed Christian. As a scholar, my special area is the study of Jesus and Christian origins. As a Christian, I am a layperson, an Episcopalian, nonliteralistic and nonexclusivistic.

I welcome the invitation for two reasons. The subject is vital for us as Christians. It matters for our understanding of Jesus and what it means to take him seriously. Moreover, I think conversation between liberal and conservative Christians is essential. I do not particularly like those labels, but I use them for shorthand purposes. Real conversation between the two is relatively rare. At stake are mutual recognition and understanding of two quite different visions of what it means to be Christian.

My contribution to this conversation consists of three main parts. First, I make some observations about the debate itself. Then I describe how I see the central issues. I conclude with a couple of issues that we as respondents were asked to address.

Observations about the Debate

Before turning to the central issues of the debate, I wish to set aside what seems to me an irrelevancy. Namely, William Craig places considerable importance on two challenges to John Dominic Crossan's work: he challenges (1) Crossan's argument that the Gospel of Peter contains very early material and (2) Crossan's acceptance of an early Secret Gospel of Mark. Craig does so in his opening

Marcus Borg is Hundere Distinguished Professor of Religion and Culture at Oregon State University.

statement, and then returns to these challenges twice, in both his rebuttal and his closing statement, suggesting that Crossan's failure to respond is significant. But these two challenges are irrelevant to the central issue of the debate. Crossan could be wrong about both, and it would make no important difference. Many scholars who are not persuaded by Crossan on either of these points nevertheless hold a position on the resurrection similar to Crossan's. That Crossan did not respond to Craig about these matters is thus without consequence.

Let me now turn to the central issues. Most central is the question, What is meant by the resurrection of Jesus? Was it physical, whatever more it might also be? Did something miraculous happen to the corpse of Jesus? Does affirming the resurrection of Jesus intrinsically involve saying, "The tomb really was empty"? Or can one meaningfully affirm the resurrection of Jesus without an empty tomb or anything special happening to the corpse of Jesus?

That this issue is the key to understanding the debate is found in the debate itself. About halfway through the dialogue section, Crossan says to Craig, "I am not denying the resurrection. You just don't like my definition of resurrection" (p. 58). For Crossan and Craig the phrase "the resurrection of Jesus" means two different things. Thus it is not that one affirms it and the other denies it. Rather, both affirm it, but each means something different.

Craig succinctly states his position in two main contentions (p. 25). They contain three claims. First, "the real Jesus rose from the dead." As the debate unfolds, it is clear what Craig means: Jesus rose physically and bodily from the tomb. Craig argues for the historical factuality of the empty tomb, speaks regularly of a physical bodily resurrection, and (when he uses phrases like "the historicity of the resurrection") means "a literal resurrection of the remains of the person in the grave" (p. 52).

Craig's second claim is that the resurrection of Jesus, understood in this way, provides "confirmation of his radical personal claims to divinity." I note that this claim presupposes that the historical Jesus did make "radical personal claims to divinity," which Crossan and I (and the majority of mainline scholars) think highly unlikely. But for the moment, I want to set that question aside and underline the way in which this statement functions in Craig's argument: the fact of the resurrection *proves* the truth of Jesus' claims to divinity. By supernaturally raising his corpse from the grave, God ratified the claims that Jesus made for himself.

Third, according to Craig, the truth of Christianity depends upon the historical factuality of a physical resurrection. As he puts it, "If Jesus did not rise, then Christianity is a fairy tale which no rational person should believe" (p. 25). Thus, for Craig, the stakes are very high: if the resurrection of Jesus did not involve the physical resurrection of a corpse, Christianity is false.

To summarize Crossan's position, I begin with a negative claim before turning to his positive claim. Crossan does not think there was an empty tomb. Indeed, he doubts that there was ever a full tomb. He thinks it more likely that what happened to Jesus' body is what typically happened to the corpses of people crucified by the Romans: it was either left on the cross for scavenger birds and dogs to devour, or buried in a common grave. Thus, for Crossan, the resurrection of Jesus has nothing to do with his corpse.

Rather, the meaning of the resurrection is that people within the early Christian movement continued to experience the "empowering presence" of Jesus after his death. This is "the fact" that lies behind the New Testament resurrection texts: "the fact was the presence of Christ and the experience thereof" (p. 47), that is, "the experienced presence of a Jesus who is dead and gone and should be out of here" (p. 64). So central is this affirmation that Crossan says, "Without that [the presence and the experience], there is no Christianity. Paul is perfectly right: without that, it's all over" (p. 47).

Finally, I note that for Crossan the resurrection of Jesus does not function as a proof, as it does for Craig. It does not prove the truth of Christianity or of claims to divinity that Jesus allegedly made.

Thus both Craig and Crossan affirm the resurrection of Jesus, but disagree about whether it involved something supernatural happening to the corpse of Jesus. Behind this disagreement are a number of other disagreements.

Two of these disagreements concern the nature and language of the Gospels. To what degree are the Gospels to be understood as straightforward historical reporting? And to what extent is the language of the Gospels (especially in the resurrection stories) metaphorical, and to what extent is it literal?

Craig basically treats the Gospels as straightforward historical documents: their purpose is to report what happened, and they generally (always?) do that reliably. In particular, he argues for the essential historical credibility of the resurrection stories.[1]

Crossan sees the Gospels as a stream of developing tradition containing earlier and later layers. As such, they contain some historical material, but that material was shaped and added to by early Christian communities in light of their own experience, their use of the Hebrew Bible, and their need to adapt the developing tradition to their own time. The Gospels are thus firsthand evidence not for the twenties and thirties of the first century, but for how the tradition had developed by the last third of the first century when they were written. They are valuable both for what they tell us about the community and for what we can, through historical reconstruction, discern about Jesus himself. On the other hand, if one sees the Gospels as straightforward historical reports, as Craig does, then the empty tomb, the appearance stories, and so forth are historical. This of course is precisely the question at issue.

Before leaving our discussion about the nature of the Gospels, we ought to note what looks like an agreement between Craig and Crossan. Craig agrees with Crossan that Mark is the earliest Gospel, that Matthew and Luke used Mark, and that there are three layers of tradition. But I wonder if this agreement is significant. In particular, is there anything in the Gospels attributed to Jesus that Craig would assign to the developing tradition and not to Jesus himself? To use the color-coded voting system of the Jesus Seminar: Is there anything in the Gospels attributed to Jesus that Craig would put in black, which represents the voice of the community rather than the voice of Jesus? Or would he put everything attributed to Jesus in red, thus indicating that whatever Matthew and Luke added to Mark was historically factual material? If so, then Craig is taking a very different view of the Gospels from that of mainline scholars, whether members of the Jesus Seminar or not.

The second disagreement concerns the extent to which the language of the resurrection stories is to be understood literally and the extent to which it is to be understood metaphorically. Craig takes them quite literally (though I, with Robert Miller, am not sure what he would say, for example, about Matthew 27:51–53, which reports

1. In addition to his remarks in the debate, see William Lane Craig, "Did Jesus Rise from the Dead?" in *Jesus under Fire,* ed. Michael J. Wilkins and J. P. Moreland (Grand Rapids: Zondervan, 1995), 141–76.

that many people were raised at the moment of Jesus' death, came out of their tombs, and then went into Jerusalem and appeared to many). On the other hand, Crossan understands the Easter stories metaphorically (it is important to realize that metaphors can be true).

Crossan's understanding is spelled out elsewhere in his treatment of two Easter stories. First, Crossan does not think the story of the two disciples on the Emmaus road in Luke 24:13–35 is an actual event which happened on the first Easter Sunday. Rather, the Emmaus story is a metaphorical narrative; it is "the metaphoric condensation of the first years of early Christian thought and practice into one parabolic afternoon." Then he concludes with two three-word sentences, both of which must be equally emphasized: "Emmaus never happened. Emmaus always happens."[2] The story is not to be understood as a historically factual account of what happened on the first Easter Sunday. Thus "Emmaus never happened." Rather, the story tells us about something that happens again and again and again—namely, the risen Christ comes to us and journeys with us, whether we know it or not. Thus "Emmaus always happens."

The second example is the story of the empty tomb, which first appears in Mark, written around 70. Mark 16:1–8 functions as Mark's Easter story. Mark has no appearance stories—only this story of the women going to the tomb, finding it empty, and being told by a young man dressed in white (presumably an angel), "He has risen, he is not here." Crossan labels this story "a parable of the resurrection, not the resurrection itself."[3] That is, the resurrection is not about an empty tomb; it is not about something happening to the corpse of Jesus. Rather, the story of the empty tomb is a powerful metaphorical affirmation that one will not find Jesus in the land of the dead, but in the land of the living. As Luke puts it in his rewriting of the words addressed to the women, "Why do you seek the living among the dead?" (Luke 24:5 RSV).

Thus, for Craig the language of the stories is literal, and for Crossan, metaphorical. This difference helps us to understand how it can be that both are affirming the resurrection, even though one of them

2. John Dominic Crossan, *Jesus: A Revolutionary Biography* (San Francisco: Harper, 1994), 197.
3. I do not know whether Crossan has said this in print, though he has said it in an interview.

denies that it involved something happening to a corpse. But both take the stories seriously, and both see the stories as true.

A third major disagreement occurs in the supernaturalism versus naturalism part of the debate. The issue is the way we are to think of God's involvement in the world. Craig affirms supernatural intervention: God directly and supernaturally intervened to raise Jesus' corpse from the grave. Indeed, it is this supernatural intervention that proves that Jesus was divine. Crossan rejects supernatural intervention; he does not think God acts that way. Rather, "the supernatural *always* operates through the screen of the natural"; it "is like the beating heart of the natural." Thus the supernatural is always present, not just in extraordinary moments; and we occasionally get "a glimpse of the permanent presence of the supernatural" (p. 45).

To sum up the differences, we might ask the two debaters what facts lie behind the New Testament texts about the resurrection. What would we have experienced had we been there? Craig would reply that we would have seen the empty tomb and the appearances of Jesus. In Crossan's view, we would have experienced the empowering presence of Jesus after his death.

A Personal Perspective

It will come as no surprise to learn that my own position is quite similar to Crossan's. Put simply, it seems to me that whether something happened to the corpse of Jesus is irrelevant to the truth of Easter. I make that statement for three reasons.

The first is a crucial distinction between two words that are often confused—resuscitation and resurrection. The meaning of resuscitation is obvious: those who are dead or believed to be dead come back to life. Such persons return to the life they had before; they need to eat and drink and sleep, and will die again someday. Resuscitation is resumption of previous existence.

Resurrection in a first-century Jewish and Christian context is a very different notion. Put compactly and somewhat abstractly, resurrection does not mean resumption of previous existence, but entry into a new kind of existence. We cannot say in detail what this is like, but it is obviously an existence very different from what we presently experience. In a sense, it is beyond the categories of life and death, for a resurrected person will not die again. There is a sense in which it is also beyond the categories of space and time; the resurrected

Christ can appear anywhere and, presumably, can appear in more than one place at the same time.

To apply this distinction to the central issue in the debate: resuscitation intrinsically involves something happening to a corpse; resurrection need not. Resurrection does not refer to the resumption of protoplasmic or corpuscular existence. To be sure, resurrection could involve something happening to a corpse, namely the transformation of a corpse; but it need not. Thus, as a Christian I am very comfortable not knowing whether the tomb was empty. Indeed, the discovery of Jesus' skeletal remains would not be a problem. It doesn't matter, because Easter is about resurrection, not resuscitation.

My second reason for affirming that the truth of Easter does not depend upon something having happened to Jesus' corpse flows out of the earliest discussion of the resurrection of Jesus in the New Testament—that provided by Paul in 1 Corinthians 15. Two features of that complex chapter are most important for the current point.

First, Paul includes himself in the list of people to whom the risen Christ appeared; implicitly, he regards his own experience as similar to the others. His own experience on the Damascus road, as we know from its threefold narration in Acts 9, 22, and 26, was a vision. I think visions can be true; unlike Craig, I never put them in the same category as hallucinations. The fundamental point here is that a vision does not require a physical body.

The second feature of 1 Corinthians 15 that is relevant to our purpose is found in the last half of the chapter, where Paul addresses the question of what the resurrection body is like. He explicitly denies that it is a physical body; instead, it is a spiritual body. I find unconvincing Craig's attempt to argue that both the spiritual body and the physical body are physical bodies, one under the control of the Holy Spirit and the other not. Not only does this argument make Paul's words say the opposite of what they seem to be saying, but (as Crossan points out) it is impossible to make Craig's interpretation apply to Jesus.

Before I leave 1 Corinthians 15, I want to note an irony. Verse 14 is often quoted by our conservative Christian brothers and sisters in support of the absolute centrality of a physical resurrection: "If Christ has not been raised, then our preaching is in vain and your faith is in vain" (RSV). But this verse is found in a chapter which explicitly denies that the resurrection body is a physical body.

My third reason has to do with the nature or character of the resurrection stories. We are back to the question of literal or metaphorical interpretation. Are we to think of these stories as reporting the kinds of events that could have been videotaped? That is another way of asking whether these stories are reporting the kinds of events that disinterested observers would have seen had they been there.

To return to the Emmaus story, do we imagine that we could have videotaped the two disciples journeying on the road and the stranger soon joining them? Could we have captured on audiotape the conversation the three of them had? Would we have been able to videotape the risen Christ vanishing from the room as the bread was broken? These questions are enough to make one begin to wonder, "Maybe it's not that kind of story." Moreover, to insist that the truth of this story depends upon its reporting the kinds of events that could have been videotaped seems very odd. And I would make a similar judgment with regard to all of the Easter stories. Their truth, and the truth of Easter itself, does not depend upon its being literal. And it does not depend upon the tomb's being empty.

For me, the truth of Easter is very simple: the followers of Jesus, both then and now, continue to experience Jesus as a living reality after his death. The post-Easter Jesus is an experiential reality. I take the phenomenology of Christian religious experience very seriously. Christians throughout the centuries have had experiences of Jesus as a living spiritual reality, a figure of the present, not simply a memory from the past. Those experiences (then and now) have taken a variety of forms, including visions and awareness of the presence of Jesus. The truth of Easter is grounded in these experiences, not in what happened (or didn't happen) on a particular Sunday almost two thousand years ago.

But the truth of Easter includes more than this. It means not simply that Jesus lives, but also that Jesus is Lord. That is, his followers experienced him after his death as having the qualities of God. Like God, he was a spiritual reality; like God, he could be experienced anywhere. To him prayers and hymns were addressed, as to God. The experiences that people had of Jesus after his death were not in the same category as experiences of one's deceased parent or spouse, from which one would not draw the inference that the parent or spouse was divine. But there was something about the experience of the risen Christ that led to that conclusion.

Easter has one further dimension of meaning that I wish to underline. Easter is God's yes to Jesus. To explain: One of the ways the early Christians talked about Jesus' death and resurrection was in terms of rejection and vindication. The crucifixion of Jesus was his rejection by "the domination system" of his day (to borrow Walter Wink's useful shorthand phrase).[4] His death was thus the domination system's no to Jesus. His resurrection was God's yes to Jesus, and God's no to the domination system of his time (and of every time). Jesus, to use the metaphorical language of the New Testament, has been exalted to God's right hand as Lord and Christ. Accordingly, Jesus is Lord, and Caesar (and every Caesar since) isn't.[5]

Concluding Matters

The editor of this volume asked the respondents to address two further questions. First, to what extent is it legitimate to distinguish between the Jesus of history and the Christ of faith? And second, can divine intervention be used in explaining the first Easter? With regard to the first question, I prefer the terms "the pre-Easter Jesus" and "the post-Easter Jesus." By the pre-Easter Jesus, I mean Jesus of Nazareth. By the post-Easter Jesus, I mean what Jesus became after his death—more specifically, the Jesus of Christian experience and tradition. Both nouns are important: the risen, living Jesus of Christian *experience*, and the Jesus of the developing Christian *tradition* as found in the Gospels and ultimately in the creeds of the church.

4. Wink is the author of a three-volume treatment of "the powers" in the New Testament. See especially volume 3, *Engaging the Powers* (Minneapolis: Augsburg Fortress, 1992). "The domination system" refers to the most common form of society for the past five thousand years: a hierarchical social order ruled by elites, marked by an economics of exploitation and a politics of oppression, and legitimated by religious ideology. In the first century, the domination system in Palestine was a combination of Roman imperial power and a native aristocracy centered in the temple.

5. Note that my exposition of Easter as God's yes to Jesus is quite different from Craig's contention that the resurrection of Jesus (understood as a physical bodily event) confirms Jesus' radical personal claims to divinity. I don't think the historical Jesus made such claims. In my view, God's yes to Jesus does not mean the confirmation of doctrinal claims made by Jesus, but God's affirmation of what Jesus was doing in a comprehensive sense: his teaching about the Way, his challenge to the domination system, and the alternative religious and social vision embodied in his willingness to partake of a meal with anyone who wished.

125

It seems to me that it is not only legitimate, but essential to distinguish between the pre-Easter Jesus and the post-Easter Jesus. If we do not make the distinction, I think we risk losing both. The need to distinguish the two is based, first, on reflection, on thinking seriously about the matter. When we do, a number of contrasts become clear:

1. The pre-Easter Jesus was a finite flesh-and-blood being who had to eat, drink, and sleep, and who could be killed. Presumably none of this is true of the post-Easter Jesus.
2. The pre-Easter Jesus was a Galilean woodworker of the peasant class. The post-Easter Jesus is King of kings and Lord of lords.
3. The pre-Easter Jesus was always in some particular place, and one had to be there in order to experience him. The post-Easter Jesus can be experienced anywhere and simultaneously by people in different places.
4. The pre-Easter Jesus is a figure of the past. By this I mean that the protoplasmic Jesus of Nazareth isn't around anymore. The post-Easter Jesus is a figure of the present.
5. In short, the pre-Easter Jesus was a flesh-and-blood reality. He was the Word and Wisdom of God made flesh. The post-Easter Jesus is a spiritual reality who has all the qualities of God; he is the Word and Wisdom of God who was flesh in Jesus of Nazareth.

The need to distinguish the two is based, second, on the nature of the Gospels as a developing tradition. As such, the Gospels contain earlier and later layers. When we separate out the layers, we discover that the earliest layers of the tradition do not contain statements in which Jesus speaks of himself as the Son of God or as the Messiah or any other exalted title. The exalted titles of Jesus (including statements like "I and the Father are one" and the great "I am" statements in John) all belong to later layers of the tradition. In short, the pre-Easter Jesus did not speak of himself as divine. Thus, as I mentioned earlier, I cannot understand the resurrection as confirmation of Jesus' radical personal claims to divinity; I don't think he made them. He was not christocentric, but theocentric, pointing not to himself, but to God.

Lest I be misunderstood, I think it is completely appropriate that the post-Easter community used the most exalted language they knew

126

to talk about the significance of Jesus. Let me use three of the great "I am" statements of John's Gospel to illustrate the point: "I am the light of the world"; "I am the bread of life"; "I am the way, the truth, and the life." I (and a large majority of mainline scholars) do not think Jesus made any of these statements; they were not part of the self-proclamation of Jesus. But I think these statements are powerfully true: they express the community's experience of the post-Easter Jesus. They experienced Jesus as the light of the world which brought them out of darkness; they experienced him as the spiritual food which fed them in the midst of their journey; they experienced him as the way which had led them from death to life. Thus the "I am" statements are the community's testimony to Jesus, not Jesus' testimony to himself.

Given the obvious differences between the pre-Easter Jesus and the post-Easter Jesus, I am puzzled by Craig's insistence that the two are (and must be) identical. I cannot imagine what he means. Does Craig really think that the resurrected Jesus has a protoplasmic body, or that the resurrected Jesus is about 5 feet tall and weighs 120 pounds (or however big Jesus of Nazareth was)? My point is not to be facetious but to ask, "Is this what Craig is talking about when he says they are identical?" And when he says at the end of his opening statement, "The Christ of faith, who lives in my heart today, is the same person who once walked the shores of Galilee" (p. 32), surely he cannot mean that the protoplasmic Jesus lives in his heart. I am sure I must have misunderstood. But I am trying to take seriously his claim that the Jesus of history and the Christ of faith are identical. If they are, how is that possible? If they aren't, how do they differ?

The second question on which the respondents were invited to reflect is whether divine supernatural intervention has a legitimate role in explaining the first Easter. I think not, for more than one reason. One problem is with the notion of supernatural intervention itself. Thinking this way tends to suppose that God is present only on exceptional occasions; most of the time God is not "here" or involved in the world. But if God sometimes intervenes from "out there," why not more often? If, for example, God could have intervened to stop the Holocaust or to stop TWA Flight 800 from exploding in the air, why didn't God do so?

A second problem is that the notion of supernatural intervention tends to privilege Christianity. It typically claims that God has acted in this tradition as God has acted in no other tradition (and specifically, in raising Jesus from the dead). I simply do not believe that God is known primarily or only in our tradition. Not only does this claim conflict with what I see in other religions, but it is inconsistent with the Christian notion of grace.

In rejecting supernatural intervention, I am not arguing for either a deistic or naturalistic position. I think paranormal things happen, including paranormal healings. But supernatural intervention is not a helpful way of explaining such events. Reality is far more mysterious than can be captured and domesticated by any system of explanation—including Christian domestications. Supernatural interventionism claims to know too much about how God acts in the world.

I conclude by noting that this debate hinges on the nature of faith. Does Christian faith mean believing that a particular thing happened two thousand years ago—namely, that Jesus' tomb was found empty, and that the most satisfactory explanation is that God supernaturally intervened to raise his corpse from the dead, and that this proves Jesus was who he said he was? Is faith to be primarily or foundationally understood as believing in the factuality of a past event? Or does Christian faith mean committing oneself to Jesus as the decisive revelation of God? For me, as a Christian, the latter seems far more important.

Resurrection Redux

Ben Witherington III

Cavils and Caveats

When I was growing up, there used to be a television program called
Dragnet. The main character in this police drama was Joe Friday.
Whenever he investigated a crime and was dealing with a witness, he
used to intone with great regularity, "Just the facts, please, just the
facts." As anyone who has ever studied written history knows, there
is no such thing as "just the facts" in historiography. It is always
facts augmented by interpretation and sometimes facts as interpretation because the facts a historian includes in his narrative are chosen by a process of critical sifting, deciding which to include and
which to exclude. This does not mean that the facts themselves are
unimportant—only that when we are dealing with historical documents there is no such thing as the plain unvarnished facts; it is always facts *and* interpretation. This in turn means that one must ask
two key questions about any historical source: (1) What things are
reported as facts? and (2) How are those facts interpreted? There can
be mistakes or distortions in either of these categories.

When we are dealing with the resurrection of Jesus, both of these
matters come into play—both the issue of facts and the issue of their
interpretation. For example, it is possible that something extraordinary really did happen to Jesus on Easter morning, but the disciples
who claimed to have seen something misunderstood the import of
the event. Or it is possible that nothing actually happened to Jesus
and his body, but the disciples thought that something did. Or it is
possible that something happened to Jesus and his body, and the disciples correctly deduced the significance of this event.

Ben Witherington III is professor of New Testament at Asbury Theological Seminary and a lifetime fellow of Robinson College, Cambridge University.

The debate between William Lane Craig and John Dominic Crossan lacks precision on these sorts of issues. But this is not the only puzzle the debate raises. At least on the surface it seems an odd thing to argue that the resurrection of Jesus proves his divinity or, somewhat less strongly, that the resurrection of Jesus proves his claims about himself, including some that suggest he saw himself as divine. Surely, it will be replied, what the resurrection proves is that Jesus was truly a human being who could die, and then be raised from the dead. Divine beings, according to this line of reasoning, don't die and have a need for resurrection. This very way of thinking brings up the difficulty of the matter. What sort of bridge can be built between Jesus' resurrection and claims about his divinity?

It is understandable and, in fact, biblical to argue that the resurrection shows that God vindicated Jesus and so vindicated his ministry and its implications. His ministry was not an exercise in deception or the raising of false hopes about the kingdom of God or the Son of man. This can be pushed a bit further to say the resurrection vindicated claims that Jesus made, whether explicit or implicit, about his role in the bringing in of God's eschatological or final saving activity. One form that this sort of argument takes can be seen in Romans 1:4, which can be translated "and was vindicated (or declared) to be Son of God in power . . . by means of resurrection from the dead." At the very least this early credal formulation suggests that Jesus was Son of God in weakness before the resurrection, but that the resurrection achieved two purposes: (1) after this event Jesus assumed new roles, such as the role of the risen Lord ruling over believers; and (2) the event itself was a sort of divine imprimatur on the life and ministry of Jesus. This, however, falls somewhat short of the notion that the resurrection proves Jesus to be divine. At most it might vindicate his claims that have a bearing on such an assessment. It must not be overlooked, however, that more than anything else the resurrection demonstrates that Jesus was truly a human being, the last or eschatological Adam, and as such, when raised, was the firstfruits of a new humanity.

I was concerned as well that nowhere in the debate was there a meaningful discussion of what one means by the term *God*. I found this a notable omission because it is not completely clear that Craig and Crossan would agree on the definition. The term *God* or *theos* in over 95 percent of its occurrences in the New Testament does not refer to either the Trinity or Jesus, but rather to God the Father, the one called Yahweh in the Old Testament. This is in no way surprising since the New Testament was written almost exclusively (with the possible exception of Luke-Acts) by Jewish Christians who continued to speak in a manner they had learned growing up. There are, however, six or seven passages in the New Testament where Jesus is probably called God (e.g., Rom. 9:5) and plenty more where he is called Lord in a divine sense (e.g., Phil. 2:9–11; cf. the Old Testament background in Isa. 45:23). It is, however, striking that none of these passages where Jesus is probably called God is found in the Synoptic Gospels. As a historian I personally have doubts that Jesus went about Galilee, saying, "Hi, I'm God, and it would be good if you would worship me." For one thing, his audience would have taken this to mean that Jesus was Yahweh, not the Son of God or the Second Person of the Trinity. Thus if we maintain that the resurrection vindicated Jesus' claims about himself, we must be clear about what those claims were. I have elsewhere argued that a reasonable case can be made that Jesus suggested that he was God's Wisdom come in the flesh, in addition to the claim that he was the Son of man.[1] This case, however, can be and is made without discussing the resurrection at all.

It is a rather different matter to say that the resurrection proved who Jesus really was—the divine Son of God—whether he made such claims or not. I would suggest that texts like Romans 1:4, which may have led Professor Craig to his way of putting the matter, in fact prove something different from Craig's formulation. Paul is not saying that the resurrection vindicated Jesus' historical or personal claims, whether explicitly or implicitly made during his ministry. Paul is saying that the resurrection revealed what God really thought about Jesus, revealed who he truly was, which was obscure before that point. In other words, Paul is not making apologetic claims of an evidentialist sort; he is making apologetic claims of an ontological sort. This is a very different matter. (One might debate, however, the possible implications of the "sign of Jonah" saying [Matt. 16:4] if one thinks it goes back to the historical Jesus.)

A further problem with the Craig-Crossan debate is that the issue of proximity is never discussed at all. No one today—at the end of

---

1. Ben Witherington III, *Jesus the Sage* (Minneapolis: Augsburg Fortress, 1993); idem, *The Christology of Jesus* (Minneapolis: Augsburg Fortress, 1990).

the twentieth century—has direct access to the facts of what happened to Jesus on Easter morning. We have direct access only to reports from the disciples of what they took to be extraordinary events. This means that at the primary level the question of the trustworthiness of the witnesses comes into play, and also, very importantly, what the disciples' intentions were when they conveyed the information we now find in the Gospels. I quite agree with Craig Blomberg that the question of the genre of the Gospels is a crucial one. But even if we cannot satisfactorily resolve this issue, we must not forget that we have documents that report these events some twenty years before even the first Gospel was written—namely Paul's letters and, of course, especially 1 Corinthians 15.

To sum up another crucial issue on which there was no clarity at all in the debate: what a person is, what a person believes himself to be, what a person claims to be, what is believed about a person by others, and what is claimed about a person by others can all be different things. For instance, it is perfectly possible that Jesus believed himself to be the Jewish Messiah and yet was mistaken. It is also possible that Jesus really was the Messiah, but he never made any claims, or at least any public ones to that effect. It is, furthermore, possible that the disciples claimed some things about Jesus that were correct assessments, but that were not grounded in anything Jesus said or did in public. Thus it is never adequate—if the question is, Who was Jesus and was he raised from the dead?—to simply deal with either just the facts or just the interpretation of facts. It is never adequate to assess just what was claimed about or even by Jesus historically. The question is, Are the claims true or not? Moreover, how do we get at the question of the veracity of the claims? How do we assess the trustworthiness of the witnesses? Pilate was right to ask, "What is truth?" We seldom deal with these deeper philosophical issues, much less the ontological issues about Jesus. I wish that Professor Craig had dealt with some of these issues in this debate as he has ably done in some of his other works.

Equally lost in this whole debate is what resurrection is, and thus what it would mean to say that Jesus rose from the dead. It would appear that Professors Craig and Crossan have rather different views on this matter.[2] It will suffice to say here that it appears that Crossan is

2. For my review of Crossan's latest offerings see *The Jesus Quest*, 2d ed. (Downers Grove, Ill.: InterVarsity, 1995), appendix I.

attempting not a change of terms, but a change of definitions of terms. The early Jews meant by "resurrection" something that happens to a human body after death, not something that happens to witnesses who encounter the raised person later. We may be uncomfortable with this definition, and some may even attempt in Bultmannian fashion a demythologizing of such notions, but we need to be clear that a hermeneutical move of this nature is not in tune with how the term was historically understood in early Judaism.

This fact becomes especially clear when we examine such phrases as *ek nekrōn egēgertai* in 1 Corinthians 15:12. Paul says that the preaching of the early church was that Christ was raised from out of the realm of the dead ones. The word *nekrōn* here does not merely mean death or the grave, but surely refers to dead persons or corpses. This is made clear in the latter half of the same verse, where Paul puts the matter a little differently, speaking of resurrection of the dead (*anastasis nekrōn*). In other words, resurrection has to do with the relationship with the persons Jesus left behind when he was raised, not the relationship he had subsequently with his followers! Jesus was raised from the dead; the other dead persons did not experience this new state of being on this occasion.

Let us consider this issue from another angle. Paul, who wrote in the early fifties but relied on traditions that went back to the earliest Christians, from whom he got his information, says, "What was of prime importance was that Jesus died for the sins of humanity and was buried; on the third day he was raised, and—subsequent to this—was seen by an enormous number of people at different times and (it would seem to be implied) in different places" (see 1 Cor. 15:3–11). Certainly Paul knew that he had seen the risen Lord at a different time and in a different place than did those witnesses he listed earlier. Now it is very difficult to doubt that for a Pharisaic Jewish Christian like Paul the sequence "died, was buried, was raised" implied not only a truly dead and buried Jesus, but also an empty tomb and a risen Lord. The Pharisaic understanding of resurrection was nothing if it was not materialistic; and more to the point, those who denied such a view of the afterlife were simply said to deny the resurrection, not to have an alternative interpretation of it (see, e.g., what is said of the Sadducees in Mark 12:18). Note, too, that Paul did not make up his understanding of what happened to Jesus; he says it was one of the most crucial things he learned from his Christian forebears and passed on to his own Corinthian converts.

Observe carefully what Paul says about the timing. The resurrection took place on a very specific occasion—on the third day after burial—but the appearances took place on a variety of occasions to various people in various locations. In short, the resurrection is not the same as the appearances of the risen Lord, never mind subjective visions of the risen Lord. Technically, no one saw or claimed to see Jesus rise from the dead, the later apocryphal Gospels notwithstanding. What the disciples saw were the results of this event: (1) an empty tomb and then (2) a risen Lord. The sequence "buried . . . raised" implied both of these for the earliest Christians.

Another factor comes into play as well in 1 Corinthians 15. Paul was a student of the Hebrew Scriptures. He knew very well the stories of Elijah and Elisha; he knew the stories of people being brought back to life by the power of God through one or another prophet. Yet Paul persists in saying that Jesus is the first example, the firstfruits, of the general resurrection. Why? Surely it is because Paul distinguished between the event of being raised from death and the state of resurrection life in a body immune to disease, decay, and death. Only Jesus had experienced the latter, and so only he could be said to have experienced the resurrection with its new mode of existence. The others had simply been brought back to their old forms of existence, not gone on to the resurrection state.

Scholars have always debated whether Paul places more emphasis on continuity or discontinuity between the present body and the resurrection body, but they have not disputed that in both cases the life spoken of is an embodied form of existence. The truth is, upon close inspection, 1 Corinthians 15 shows that Paul wished to affirm both continuity and discontinuity between the two states. In both situations it is the same person who has life in an embodied state. On the other hand, in the resurrection one has a body that is imperishable, glorious, powerful, and totally animated and empowered by the Holy Spirit.

Now Paul was perfectly aware that some persons' bodies, being long dead, were no longer extant. The Jews often visited their family tombs and sometimes placed remains in bone boxes or ossuaries when the flesh had totally decayed, a practice early Christians also followed. I would suggest that this knowledge of decomposition explains why Paul does not really speak of or use the phrase "resurrection of the body," but deals instead with the concept "resurrection in the body" or "the resurrection body." If the metaphor of seed and plant (15:37–42) conveys any meaning, it suggests more discontinuity than continuity, though the latter is not denied. In other words, the earliest Christians were not so naive as to believe that it was necessarily the same body refurbished that appeared later. But in the case of Jesus there was a body to be raised that provided the material starting point for a transformation that resulted in a live person in a resurrection body. In other words, it was much the same with Jesus as it will be for those who Paul says will be living and thus transformed when Christ returns (15:50–55). Thus our earliest evidence about resurrection and Jesus does not encourage us to think of the early Christians' merely having visions or spiritual experiences of Jesus after he died. Our earliest records make far stronger, and to the Greco-Roman world more startling, claims than that (see Acts 17:31–32).

Perhaps one example of an early critique of the vision theory is in order. It is telling that in assessing the women's testimony about the empty tomb the male disciples concluded (1) that it was an idle tale (Luke 24:11) and (2) that at most one could speak of a vision of angels (Luke 24:23). Bearing in mind that the report in Luke 24:19–23 is given by disciples who are leaving Jerusalem and speaking in the past tense about having had hope that Jesus was the one to redeem Israel, we conclude that no mere visions or reports of visions of supernatural beings or reports of empty tombs were going to change these discouraged disciples' mental state. Only an encounter with the risen Lord would do that. There is in this narrative a quality that critiques the male leadership of the early church and at the same time shows that mere visions or claims of visions were not what changed the lives of the disciples.

This brings us to the Gospels themselves. Here, as in 1 Corinthians 15, the materiality of the risen Jesus is brought out in various ways. The important point to be noted is that we have several independent testimonies to this effect, and thus by the criterion of multiple attestation there is a high likelihood that this motif goes back to the earliest oral accounts about the encounters with Jesus after his death. In the Markan account, for instance, even if one insists that Mark 16:8 is the end of this Gospel (a point I would dispute, for I think the original ending is missing in Mark), we nevertheless find the words, "He has been raised; he is not here. Look, there is the place they laid him" (v. 6 NRSV). This is an account that associates resurrection with something that happened to Jesus' material body so that it was no longer present in the tomb. Or consider Matthew 28:9, where we read that the women clasped Jesus' feet and worshiped him. Again resurrection involves a material being who can be touched. Luke puts the matter even more strongly. Jesus says, "Look at my hands and my feet; see that it is I myself. Touch me and see; for a ghost does not have flesh and bones as you see that I have" (Luke 24:39 NRSV). The same point arises in the accounts found in John 20. In short, all four Gospels stress the materiality of what resurrection entailed for Jesus. The question is, Why?

It is sometimes suggested that the stress on the physicality of the resurrection of Jesus is pure apologetics. I have always been mystified by this claim. If the Gospels were written in the last third of the first century when the church not only had a viable Gentile mission but was well on the way to becoming a largely Gentile community, why in the world would a group trying to attract Gentiles make up a resurrection story, much less emphasize the material resurrection of Jesus? This notion was not a regular part of the pagan lexicon of the afterlife at all, as even a cursory study of the relevant passages in the Greek and Latin classics will show. Indeed, as Acts 17 suggests, pagans were more likely than not to ridicule such an idea. I can understand the apologetic theory if, and only if, the Gospels were directed largely to Pharisaic Jews or their sympathizers. I know of no scholar, however, who has argued such a case.

We are thus left with the fact that the earliest Christians, proponents of a missionary religion, nevertheless stressed a material notion of resurrection, including a material notion of what happened to their founder at Easter. I submit that the best explanation for this phenomenon is that something indeed must have happened to Jesus' body, and he must have been in personal and visible contact with his followers after Easter.

If it were merely the case that something happened to Jesus' body at Easter, it could easily have been assumed that he was taken up into heaven like an Elijah or an Enoch. The fact is, as the Gospel traditions such as John 20:2 make evident, an empty tomb by itself was subject to a variety of interpretations including graverobbing. The empty-tomb story by itself would not likely have generated the belief in a risen Jesus. There must have also been appearances of the risen Lord to various persons.

Perhaps here is the place to say something about various alternative theories of the resurrection. There are several problems with the suggestions that the disciples were victims of hallucination, that their experience was the ultimate example of wish-projections, or that they merely saw visions. First, on all accounts the disciples doubted, deserted, denied Jesus at the end, with the possible exception of some of the female followers of Jesus. They were hardly in a psychological condition to produce a fantasy about a risen Jesus. Their hopes had been utterly shattered by his crucifixion less than three days before. Second, it will not do to suggest a mass hallucination because all the traditions we have suggest that Jesus appeared at different times and places to different persons, last of all to Paul. I know of no basis for the notion of a contagious hallucination. Third, it is hardly believable that the earliest Christians would have made up the notion that Jesus appeared first to some women. Search as we may, we find no extended discussion in the Gospels of a personal appearance to Peter or to James the brother of the Lord. We do, however, have stories about the appearance or appearances to the leading female disciples. In the patriarchal world in which the earliest Christians lived, it is frankly not believable that a missionary-minded group would have made up such a story. Nor, against Crossan, is there any basis for the suggestion that these appearance stories were largely generated out of the Old Testament, which hardly mentions the notion of resurrection from the dead. In other words, the historical Christian witness as we have it is strongly against Crossan's attempt to redefine "resurrection."

Resurrection and Reconstruction

Though it is sometimes a difficult distinction for some to understand, there is a considerable difference between the historical Jesus and the historically reconstructible Jesus. By the historical Jesus, I mean Jesus as he actually was two thousand years ago. If historical reconstruction is done properly, then the historically reconstructed Jesus will be at best a subset of the historical Jesus. The historical Jesus could also be called the real Jesus, except for the fact that in this particular debate Crossan apparently wishes to call only the Jesus of two thousand years of Christian faith the real Jesus. Now this real Jesus of Crossan's amounts to the Jesus that Christians have always believed in, but is distinguishable from the earthly Jesus, whom I call the historical Jesus. The problem with Crossan's "real Jesus" concept is that it speaks only of what others have believed and still believe about Jesus. It does not speak of who Jesus actually was. Furthermore, Crossan is notably shy about saying anything regarding the relationship of the earthly Jesus and his real Jesus. This is problematic especially when we are dealing with a historical religion like Christianity. If who we believe Jesus to be is not consistent with who he was and who he became by means of the resurrection, namely the risen Lord, then we have a problem of credibility.

Whether Christianity stands or falls depends on certain historical facts—not merely historical claims, but historical facts. Among these facts that are most crucial to Christian faith is the fact of Jesus' resurrection from the dead. The Christian faith is not mere faith in faith—ours or someone else's—but rather a belief about the significance of certain historical events. Paul was quite right to say that if Christ has not been raised, Christians are the most pitiable of all human beings. They are believers in a lie if Christ is not raised. If Christ is not raised, the way we may look at God also changes.

The resurrection demonstrates that there is a power in the universe greater than death—namely, the life-giving power of God. This power means not merely that God is capable of creating new life from scratch, but that he is able to re-create life which has died. The resurrection means that God, not death, has the last word about human ends and destiny. To date, there has been only one example of resurrection on this planet; and therefore, if Jesus is not raised, we have no concrete evidence that God really is almighty to save a person from the clutches of death and its realm. From this point of view, the resurrection of Jesus is the most important event in all of human history. It demonstrates what God is capable of beyond all human limitations and expectations.

Christian hope has sometimes been caricatured as a hope for pie in the sky by and by. This is indeed a caricature, for the earliest Christians understood that Christian hope is grounded in what God has already accomplished in Christ; it therefore looks forward to the future with a reasonable expectation that what God did for Jesus, God can also do for us. It was Paul's view that Christ's history is the Christian's destiny. This is still the orthodox Christian's hope today.

It is notable how very little the New Testament says about dying and going to heaven. But when the matter is discussed (e.g., in 2 Cor. 5:1–10), Paul makes clear that life without a body in heaven is by no means his ultimate hope or expectation in regard to how he will spend eternity. Indeed, Paul calls life in heaven without a body nakedness, which to an early Jew was hardly the most desirable state of affairs. While it is true that under the influence of Greek thought medieval Christianity often substituted immortality of the soul for the New Testament doctrine of resurrection of the body, this is frankly not what the majority of New Testament passages are speaking of when they speak about the afterlife. Indeed, it could be said that the New Testament sees life in heaven without a body as only an interim condition.[3] For resurrection is something that will happen in the earthly realm to real persons who have died. It is not an event in some other realm (e.g., heaven) that is immune from historical scrutiny and evaluation. It is noteworthy that Jerome Murphy-O'Connor has recently suggested that the whole reason Christians believed in the immortality of the human personality beyond death at all was their belief that a person had to be there for God in Christ to raise up on the last day.[4] How very different this is from what one usually hears today about dying and going to heaven.

It is a sign of the weakness of a particular position when claims about Jesus or the resurrection are removed from the realm of historical reality and placed in a purely subjective realm of personal belief or some realm that is immune from human scrutiny. I would suggest that this sort of approach does Jesus and the resurrection no service and no justice. It is a ploy of desperation to suggest that Christian faith would not be much affected if Jesus were not actually raised from the dead in space and time. This is the approach of those desperate to maintain their faith even at the expense of historical reality or the facts. When such persons give up on the historical foundations of the Christian faith, they have in fact given up on the possibility of any real continuity between their own faith and that of a Peter, a Paul, a James, a John, a Mary Magdalene, or a Priscilla.

3. Ben Witherington III, *Jesus, Paul, and the End of the World* (Downers Grove, Ill.: InterVarsity, 1992).

4. Jerome Murphy-O'Connor, *Paul: A Critical Life* (Oxford: Clarendon, 1996).

Whatever may be said about such an approach today, a non-historical bullet-proof faith is not the faith that the early Christians lived and died for. It is in fact a rather gnostic or docetic approach to Christian faith. Strangely enough, it is one that I find exists in some forms even in the most conservative of Christian circles. With regularity I am confronted with students who ask why it matters that this or that event happened as long as they find their own personal faith experiences to be satisfying and transforming. The answer is that if we retreat into pure subjectivity, then there is no objective criterion by which we may determine the difference between a heartwarming experience sent by God and mere heartburn, between things that are good for us and things that merely feel good. "Resurrection Lite," or the resurrection of pure metaphor or even pure otherworldliness, was not what the earliest Christians believed in. "Less intellectually filling, still tastes great," was not their motto. They had an interest in historical reality, especially the historical reality of Jesus and his resurrection, because they believed that their faith, for better or worse, was grounded in it.

Nor was this faith something that was conjured up years or even generations later than Jesus' lifetime. Paul was in direct contact with various eyewitnesses of the life, death, and resurrection appearances of Jesus. It is striking that nowhere in his letters does he have to argue with other major Christian leaders about his views of the resurrection and the risen Lord. Indeed he suggests in Romans 10, Philippians 2, and elsewhere that the earliest confession of the Christians was "Jesus is the risen Lord." Furthermore, he suggests in 1 Corinthians 15:1–5 that the earliest Christians also had very particular beliefs about the end of Jesus' earthly life and the transition to his present heavenly state as risen and exalted Lord. Paul wrote 1 Corinthians 15 within twenty-five years of Jesus' death, while various of the original eyewitnesses were still around to correct him. The silence of his Christian peers on this issue compared to their criticism of his views on the law (see Galatians) is deafening. It shows where the common ground truly lay.

Thus it will not do to suggest that the passion and resurrection narratives in the Gospels were largely constructed out of the Old Testament. The outline of and some vignettes from these narratives can already be found in Paul's letters in places like 1 Corinthians 11 and 15. Furthermore, what actually caused the earliest Christians to race

140

back to their sacred Scriptures was the need to interpret the significance of the startling things that happened to Jesus at the close of his earthly career—his shocking crucifixion and then his equally startling resurrection. The earliest Christians did not first find these events in the Old Testament prophecies and then create new narratives out of those prophecies. The proof is that the original contexts of the Hebrew Scriptures used to interpret the key final events of Jesus' life would never have suggested any such interpretation to a reader who had not heard of Jesus' life, death, and resurrection. I know of no evidence that non-Christian early Jews were looking for a resurrected Messiah, and in fact the evidence that they were looking for a crucified one is also very doubtful.[5]

Certainly one of the most shocking aspects of Professor Crossan's analysis of the resurrection narratives in the Gospels is his conclusion that "Easter never happened. Easter always happens." He, of course, does not say this in this particular debate; indeed, his approach in this debate raises questions about some of the things he has written, for instance, in books like *Who Killed Jesus?* Perhaps we may hope he is open to changing his mind on some of these matters.

One issue in particular I would want to press with Crossan on the "Easter never happened" front is the substance of the stories of the women's visit to the tomb and the subsequent appearances of Jesus to them. Crossan's dismissal of the essential historical substance of these narratives located at the tomb is especially surprising in view of how the testimony of women was evaluated in patriarchal cultures in the first century A.D.[6] C. H. Dodd once suggested that the story of Mary Magdalene at the tomb is one of the most self-authenticating stories in all the Gospels. In his view, it has all the elements of the personal testimony of an eyewitness. First of all, given what the tradition said about Mary Magdalene's past (Luke 8:2), it is hardly credible that the earliest Christians would have made up a story about Jesus' appearing first to her. Second, it is not credible that a later Christian hagiographer would have had her suggest that perhaps Jesus' body had been stolen from the tomb. Third, it is not be-

5. See Ben Witherington III, *The Many Faces of the Christ* (New York: Crossroad, 1998).

6. See Ben Witherington III, *Women in the Ministry of Jesus*, Society for New Testament Studies Monograph Series 51 (Cambridge: Cambridge University Press, 1984).

lievable that later reverential Christians would have suggested that the first eyewitness mistook Jesus for a gardener! The portrait of Mary and her spiritual perceptiveness is hardly flattering here. Fourth, it is not believable that the early Christians would have created the idea that Jesus commissioned Mary to go proclaim the Easter message to the Eleven. On this last point we have the clear support of 1 Corinthians 15, where we see that the testimony of women to the risen Lord, if not totally eliminated in the official witness list (they might be alluded to in the reference to the appearance to the five hundred), is clearly sublimated.

Thus it is simply not believable that early Christians made up stories about women and particularly Mary Magdalene as the first and foremost validating witnesses of the risen Lord. This is especially not credible considering the fact that the writers of the Gospels like other early Christians were hoping for more converts. "These are written so that you may come to believe," says the fourth Evangelist at the end of John 20 (v. 31 NRSV). A more serious reckoning with the resurrection narratives, especially John 20, but also the information we find in Mark 16, Matthew 28, and to a lesser degree Luke 24, is necessary if we really want to get at the heart of the earliest forms of the stories about that first Easter and thus get at the bottom of what happened on that first Easter Sunday morning. I submit that these stories cannot be ignored. It is not convincing to appeal to Mark 16:8 as the original ending for such stories, as that is an argument from silence, not substance. In fact, even if we were to stop at Mark 16:8, the resurrection and empty tomb are clearly proclaimed, and the "going before you into Galilee" motif suggests the appearances were not limited to Jerusalem, but also occurred in Galilee.

Metaphorically Speaking

One of the categories of language which seems to come up in the discussion rather regularly is that of metaphorical speech or, as it is sometimes called, figurative language. At several points in the debate the literal-versus-figurative issue is raised, but in fact not discussed. It seems, however, to be assumed that wherever a description is literal or a text is interpreted literally, facts must be involved, and that, on the other hand, if metaphors, similes, or figurative language in general is used, then facts are not—or are not likely to be—involved. I find this whole approach quite wooden and unhelpful. On the one hand, even cold facts can be described in metaphors or figurative language. On the other hand, a literal description or interpretation can be given of some fictional object or person.

My particular concern is with metaphors used to describe real events. For example, some years ago shortly after an earthquake in Oakland, California, one person's description of the experience quoted the psalmist's imagery of the hills skipping like lambs (Ps. 114:4). This is certainly apt in the sense that the hills and bridges and buildings were jumping up and down when the main force of the quake hit. In this modern use of the psalm, metaphorical language describes a very real event in space and time. The question, then, is not whether one finds metaphorical language in the birth narratives or resurrection narratives (e.g., the Holy Spirit overshadowed Mary—obviously the Spirit does not literally cast a shadow); the question is, What sort of use is made of metaphorical language? It can't be simply assumed that once one finds metaphors, one has found fiction.

While we're on this subject, I also object to the narrow use of the term *literal* in the debate. To my way of thinking, once one determines the genre of a particular piece of literature, a "literal" interpretation is one that construes the text in accord with the literary and historical conventions of that genre. Now perhaps one would prefer to call such an interpretation a "proper" interpretation rather than a "literal" one, but it seems odd to say that one can't give a literal interpretation to something that involves a metaphor.

In fact, one *can* give a literal interpretation to a passage that involves figurative language; some cases are justified and some cases not. If one were to interpret a parable as a literal description of some real event in space and time, one would likely be incorrect. But in the case of a historical text that uses a metaphor or simile to make the description of an actual event more vivid, one is on very different grounds. Here metaphor is used as part of the vehicle of reporting the literal event. One will be justified in referring to the event itself as actual, but must not insist that the description is historically accurate in every particular.

Then of course there is the case of literalistic interpretations of texts not meant to be read that way. For example, once when hitch-hiking in the mountains of North Carolina, I received a ride from an elderly couple who were flat-earthers. That is, they refused to believe the world is round. When I asked why, they replied, "Because it says in the Book of Revelation that the four angels will stand upon the four corners of the earth [see Rev. 7:1], which would be impossible if the world is round." The problem in this case was that the couple did not realize that apocalyptic literature never intended to teach cosmology or the shape of the earth. They mistook a figurative description for a literal one. A proper or literal reading of the text with an understanding of its genre and metaphorical character would have ruled out their conclusion.

I am also unhappy with the debate on naturalism versus supernaturalism, though not because I agree with Crossan that the supernatural always operates through the screen of the natural or is like the beating heart of the natural. That sounds far too much like pantheism or panentheism to me. It is simply not the case that miracles are always there, if by miracles we mean what the Gospels call miracles. Sometimes people do not get cured. Sometimes nothing special happens, and yet on other occasions it does. A miracle is a sporadic or periodic event, not merely a glimpse by faith of the ever-present eternal. Miracles are not, in the first place, acts of faith but events understood through faith. They do in fact happen even if no one understands at the time. Mark's Gospel is repeatedly concerned to remind us that Jesus did miracles and frequently the disciples did not understand them; indeed, frequently the one being healed did not understand or have faith. Often faith follows the miracle, not precedes it.

I suspect that the heart of the problem for Crossan is revealed toward the end of the debate when he says that his theological presupposition is that God does not intervene in human affairs from time to time, say, at Lourdes when a healing occurs (p. 61). His assumption appears to be that the divine is always present. From a theological point of view, however, I must insist that the Bible is a book based on the assumption that God does indeed intervene in human history over and over again. In particular, various early Christians believed that the incarnation of God in Jesus Christ was a very specific event that occurred at a very specific time and place. Equally, they believed that resurrection happened to Jesus in A.D. 30 in a way that it had never happened before or, we may say, since. Neither the incarnation nor the resurrection was a perpetual occurrence. Both were in fact events distinguishable from the notion that all the universe can be present to God at once—so vast is God—and from the notion of the ongoing presence of God's Spirit in the life of the believer.

Intervention in space and time also means that there are times when there are no miracles and even times when human beings experience the absence of the presence of God. Indeed, some texts even speak of a place where one can experience the absence of the presence of God forever—namely, hell. Much more can be said along these lines, but space will not permit. It will be seen that the debate scared up far more rabbits than it bagged, but this is useful, for it means we still have much more to discuss in the future.

My cursory response to the debate is intended to be more suggestive than definitive. Much more needs to be said. Suffice it to say at this point that I found the debate had some interesting moments but often failed to grasp the nettle. I have tried to suggest how and on what terms the discussion could be carried forward. Resurrection is not merely a concept or a state of mind or heart. It is a historical event, and in the life of Jesus it is an epoch-making event. It tells us that God's evaluation of Jesus and his ministry differs from the evaluation made by many moderns, including various members of the Jesus Seminar. I see no good historical reasons to disagree with the Almighty's evaluation.

8

Concluding Reflections

Reflections on a Debate

John Dominic Crossan

To understand texts or speakers from the early first or late twentieth century, some information about purpose and intention is crucial. Sometimes, as in that former case, purpose can only be inferred from the text itself, and sometimes, as in the latter case, it can be inferred from the text or offered by the author. Here, then, as clearly and honestly as I can, let me state both my purpose in entering the debate and, in the light of that purpose, my thoughts about it now.

Dick Staub has a show called *Chicago Talks* on WYLL in Elk Grove Village, Illinois. On three separate occasions—in 1992, 1994, and 1995—he invited me to discuss one of my recent books. Each time an opposing scholarly opinion was represented either in person or on the phone. Everything was completely courteous, appropriate, and proper. Dick is both personally honorable and professionally ethical, and against that background I agreed immediately to join in the proposed debate with Bill Craig. I was also offered veto power over three later changes, but agreed quite readily to them all. Would it be all right to have the debate at Moody Memorial Church, which would be big enough for about three thousand people and still not prohibitively expensive? Of course. Would it be all right to have Bill Buckley Jr. as moderator? Of course. Then, at the very last moment, came this: Bill Buckley understood that he would both moderate and participate. He would not come otherwise. Was that all right? Of course. I knew that Bill Buckley would not be neutral or impartial in the debate, but I considered that a minor detail. I still do. There were much more important issues at stake, and I trusted then and now the complete integrity of Dick Staub.

I consider it important that representatives from the full spectrum of Christianity be in some humane conversation with one another. I see various groups claiming exclusive authenticity for themselves and exercising rhetorical genocide on the others. (See how these Christians hate one another.) I hoped then and still hope now for "the ultimate ecumenism," intra-Christian dialogue to put an end to the disgraceful situation that Christians will talk to any and all others before they talk to one another. But, above all else, I wanted to get down to the theological-historical interface where divergent presuppositions will necessarily involve surface disagreements. I did not want to spend my time on surface disagreements, however, where there was little chance that Bill Craig or I would change one another's opinion. The reason was not that we are unequally logical or rational. That would be too easy an explanation. The reason was that we start from a different theological-historical nexus. So I did not intend to change his basic theological-historical nexus, but to get our diversity out in the open as clearly as possible. I wanted to see if I could explain to a predominantly conservative Christian audience how a liberal Christian like myself sees the Gospels in general and the historical Jesus in particular. I hoped that the audience might be able, first, to glimpse the integrity of two opposing Christian viewpoints and, second, to glimpse where theological agreement might be possible despite historical disagreement.

Now imagine, if you will, three different types of Christians whom I will label simply Group A, Group B, and Group C. Group A believes that everything in the Gospels that can be taken literally and historically should be so taken. I consider that to be a theological presupposition based on an a priori belief about what divine inspiration must do. Members of Group A themselves might see it as an a posteriori historical judgment or even as some delicate interaction between theology and history. I do not, emphatically do not, judge it invalid even if it is a totally theological presupposition.

Group B thinks that some stories that could be taken literally were intended to be and should be taken symbolically instead. I myself belong to Group B and consider its position to be a historical judgment based on an a posteriori experience of what divine inspiration has done. I locate Bob Miller and Marcus Borg in that same group. Bob gives the reasons for and Marcus the results of reading the resurrection texts according to Group B's basic principle.

Group A might well say that Group B's position is simply an alternative, a priori theological presupposition. They could argue that, since I believe God can work as well through fiction as through fact, I find both categories in the Gospels. I might respond that, since they believe God works through fact, they find only fact in the Gospels. (We are not, of course, debating whether stories *by* Jesus could be parables, that is, sacred fiction. On that we all agree. We are debating whether stories *about* Jesus could be parables, that is, sacred fiction. Examples would be the triumphal entry, the burial by Joseph of Arimathea, and the discovery of the empty tomb.) That is an honest discussion which deserves to be continued, and it is my hope that it can be continued. Indeed, it was to foster such discussion that I agreed to participate in the debate. In the process of discussion, we will be required to compare those presuppositions about theological-historical interaction that divide us. And that will require abstention from caricature on both sides. It does not help to argue that one's opponents are less logical, rational, or critical than oneself when, in fact, they are just as logical, rational, and critical but work from divergent presuppositions.

The discussion between Groups A and B can proceed on two levels. One level is the presentation, comparison, and discussion of the theological and historical presuppositions just mentioned. And the result of that necessary conversation may be no more and no less than an appreciation of the integrity of an opponent's position. Understanding rather than conversion may well be the outcome on that level, and that will be quite satisfactory. The second level has to do with agreeing to disagree on presuppositions and asking instead about meaning and the practical consequences thereof. For example, let us say that representatives from Groups A and B disagree on whether Jesus' triumphal entry into Jerusalem was factual or fictional, that is, actually happened in history or was created in the Gospels. They could continue to argue that point forever and might well get nowhere. But what if they eliminated historicity from consideration and discussed meaning? Could they agree that, whether as historical action or Gospel creation, that story portrays Jesus' dominion

149

as antiroyal and anti-imperial, as almost a lampoon on how earthly power normally operates? And, if they agreed on that, what about power in the world we live in today?

The discussion between Groups A and B, be it on the level of theoretical presuppositions or on the level of practical consequences, should be an honest and honorable activity. There is, however, a third Christian group with which I admit immediately that I have very great difficulty in dealing. I find it procedurally dishonest because, in the argot of the moment, it talks the talk of Group B but walks the walk of Group A. I repeat, once more for emphasis, that I consider both Group A and Group B to be honest alternatives, but Group C should not exist at all. Group C agrees with Group B in theory but differs from it in practice. It is very slow or even reluctant to decide in the concrete on what is historical and what is symbolical. It often seems to take back in actual practice what it asserts in theoretical possibility. Case after case comes out as actual and historical, especially when anything of consequence is concerned.

Of course, whenever any of these groups interact, there will be some problems. It is hard, for example, for Group A not to describe Group B as evil and destructive. It is hard for Group B not to describe Group A as stupid and dogmatic. They often waste one another's time in debating whether this or that unit is historical. They literally cannot hear one another. As a member of Group B, I understand that situation and can only attempt to explain to Group A, if it cares, how I can be a believing Christian and still find very much of the Gospel accounts about Jesus to be traditional and evangelical rather than original and historical. Such, for me, is the nature of the Gospels. Were I in debate with Group A, a position which I consider wrong but whose integrity I respect, the only fruitful discussion would be on theological positions or practical consequences. Why, I might ask my opponent, is God restricted to giving only factual information? If Jesus made up parables about God, why can his followers not make up parables about Jesus? And, more importantly, whether we take, for example, the triumphal entry as factual or fictional, historical or symbolical, what difference does it make for our interpretation of the story? What if we agreed to disagree here on historicity, but went on to discuss interpretation? For example, is the kingdom of God or the kingship of Jesus about power and domination or about justice and persuasion?

There are even disagreements between members of the same group. Bob Miller, for example, has argued powerfully elsewhere that Jesus' symbolic destruction of the temple is not historical. I disagree and think it actually happened. I am sure, however, that our debate is within Group B. Neither of us has a theological presupposition, either theoretical or practical, one way or the other on the subject. He could change my mind and I his on that or any other historical question. I would say the same for Marcus Borg on, for instance, the burial of Jesus. If we debated its historicity, I would be sure of a straightforward historical rather than crypto-theological argument. It is, I confess once again, with Group C that I have the most serious problems; in fact, I hope that it does not exist at all. If I were in debate with members of that hypothetical group, I would not know for sure whether I was in a straightforward historical argument or in a theological argument disguised as a historical one. Now I have a very simple test to find out whether an opponent is in Group A or C. If in Group A, one should just say so, and we can get on with the debate on that presumption. Those who are not in Group A should give a list of words or deeds of Jesus that they think are not historical but symbolical, metaphorical, parabolical, figurative, or any other term that could be used to describe sacred and divinely inspired fiction. Those not in Group A should also put in print (as I have put in print) what they think comes from the historical Jesus, what comes from the ongoing Christian tradition, and what comes from the creativity of the Evangelists. This test will detect those who while claiming to accept the theoretical and methodological principles of Group B, negate them practically and consistently in case after case. Such people are, in other words, Group A disguised as Group B.

It should be clear that my problem is not at all with theological presuppositions. I have already accepted the integrity of Group A. The problem is masking theological debates as historical ones. Let me illustrate from Craig Blomberg's response: "A careful comparison of the Synoptics makes it abundantly clear that the Evangelists *selected* what they believed was relevant for the particular Christian communities that they were addressing. . . . But none of this variation requires us to conclude that the Evangelists *distorted*, *falsified*, or *invented* history at any point" (pp. 104–5, italics added). I spent the 60s in excruciatingly detailed comparison of the Gospels in parallel columns, word by word and unit by unit, day by day and year by year. I was in a monastery, by the way, and alternative diversions were rather limited. I was testing and establishing for myself that Matthew and Luke used Mark as one major source, that the Q Gospel was their other documentary source, and that John was dependent on those earlier Gospels at least for the narrative frames at start and finish. Those genetic relationships were thereafter my historical presuppositions and, if wrong today or disproved tomorrow, everything I have done on the historical Jesus would need review. My presuppositions could be falsified, for example, by a child playing soccer on the edge of the Libyan Desert and kicking open a jar that contains a very primitive Gospel displaying aspects of all four canonical ones.

It is, in fact, primarily from studying Matthew's and Luke's work on Mark, not to speak of John's possible work on all of them, that I concluded what a Gospel is, how it works, and how creative an Evangelist can be. Matthew, for example, does not simply "select" from some unspecified general tradition. He omits from, adds to, and changes his Markan source, including the very words and deeds of Jesus. Scholars are quite free to deny that conclusion, but they are not free to caricature it. Even the claim that a Gospel created an event out of whole cloth does not warrant the judgment that the Evangelists "*distorted, falsified,* or *invented* history," which are profoundly negative and inaccurate terms. Jesus' parable about the good Samaritan, even if created there and then, does not do any of those things, and neither do, for example, the narratives about the triumphal entry, the burial by Joseph of Arimathea, and the discovery of the empty tomb, even if they were created by Mark or someone before him. None of those three pejorative descriptions apply unless, of course, one has already established that the Gospels are always presented as historical descriptions.

Finally, let me discuss two specific items, historical mistakes and generic frameworks. In both cases I am speaking of individual units and not of whole Gospels. First, with regard to historical mistakes, that is, instances of a biblical author's intending to give historical information but getting it wrong. We all agree that the Bible is the inspired Word of God. The Gospels, therefore, are absolutely true-as-Word-of-God. Is it possible that true-as-Word-of-God could tolerate some historical mistakes? I think Group A would probably say no. Group B would say yes and give some examples. Group C might say yes in theory but no to every individual case suggested as an example. A standard and beaten-to-death case is Luke's association of the birth of Jesus with a census under the Syrian governor Quirinius. Does that mistake in any way invalidate the Gospel as true-as-Word-of-God? Of course not. But it warns me that God is not concerned with protecting inspired writers on matters peripheral to the point at hand. God may help them to be good Christians but not to be accurate historians. That requires proper homework, not divine inspiration.

Allow me, tongue in cheek, to exemplify my point from the respondents to the debate. Craig Blomberg says that "a recent example of scholarly skepticism [about the burial story] appears in" the *Biblica* article "Did Joseph of Arimathea Exist?" That is simply incorrect. The article actually affirms the historicity of the burial story, especially against my own proposals. That is simply a passing homework mistake that does not invalidate the general point Blomberg is making, namely, that there is some debate about the historicity of the burial narrative. A similar factual mistake appears in Ben Witherington's statement that "one of the most shocking aspects of Professor Crossan's analysis of the resurrection narratives in the Gospels is his conclusion that 'Easter never happened. Easter always happens.'" That also is simply incorrect. What I said was that "Emmaus never happened. Emmaus always happens." Witherington, who disagreed with my conclusion, cited it incorrectly. Marcus, who agreed with it, cited it correctly. The Emmaus narrative in Luke 24 is not a historical story about a one-time event on Easter Sunday afternoon, but a symbolical story about all-time Christian faith, that is, about experiencing the risen Lord partially in biblical exegesis and fully in eucharistic meal. We biblical scholars make mistakes, and ancient inspired authors also made mistakes.

Second, with regard to generic frameworks. My example here is polemics. We have all learned to take political invective with large doses of salt in election years. Is there such a thing as true-as-invective, true-as-polemics? Or, as in this country, are people both motivated and sickened by such political devices? Can an inspired Gospel use them? Can it place on the lips of Jesus attacks that he never uttered but that articulate later Christian controversies? Does the genre of political invective exist in the inspired Word of God? In this case I do not know what Group A or B or C might say, so I answer only for myself. Yes, it does, and it must be understood as such.

In the first century, Christian Jews, then relatively few and powerless, lashed out against other Jews whom they opposed and who opposed them. Jesus in Matthew 23 thunders woes of corporate character-assassination against the Pharisees. The Pharisaic responses are not recorded. In John 8:44 Jesus tells a group of Jews, "You are from your father the devil"; and they respond in 8:48, "You are a Samaritan and have a demon" (NRSV). Equal opportunity invective, in that case. *Vituperatio* was an ancient and honorable genre, and its function was the rhetorical destruction of an opponent. I am sorry our inspired texts contain such material and extremely sorry about the later uses to which it was put. But its presence warns me that when the Holy Spirit and the human heart interact, some very nasty stuff can receive divine authentication. Whether the attacks I have mentioned actually came from Jesus is not my present concern. They are, in any case, in our sacred texts and demand our attention. If everything in there is factually true, then the Pharisees are so-and-sos and the Jews are such-and-such. But if everything, that is, every individual unit, must be understood within its generic framework, then the invective and vituperation must be taken as telling us facts not about the Pharisees or the Jews, but about the communities of Matthew and John.

That is only one small example of what must be done over and over again in case after case of reading the Gospels comparatively. Let me once again put my tongue in cheek and move from ancient to modern vituperation. Here is a sentence from Craig Blomberg about me: "Not least because of his voluminous publishing and frequent media appearances, Crossan's perspectives have influenced not only the Jesus Seminar, but a considerable scattering of unpublished or little-known university professors in departments of religious studies around the country." Invective, first-century or twentieth-century style, is about the sender, not the receiver.

My purpose in the debate, as mentioned earlier, was to see if two divergent Christian positions can talk to one another. William Craig and I represented, respectively, Group A and Group B. I hope that dialogue between us is still possible. I can no longer, however, accept Group C as honorable (if it exists, and I hope it does not) until it gives me some examples of what in the Gospels it finds unhistorical.

Did the tradition and the Evangelists create some of the words and deeds they attributed to Jesus? Did they, as was accepted in ancient biography, create speech-in-character and event-in-character? Did they, in other words, create words and deeds which quite deliberately and consciously say, "This is what our Jesus would have said and done in such a situation had it occurred when he was alive"? Anyone whose answer is no is in Group A, and we can dialogue on that basis. If the answer is yes, I want examples and as many as possible so I can see the principles at work in the selection. Lacking multiple examples, I will consider anyone who answers yes to be a member of Group A in disguise. In that case, I doubt if any dialogue is useful.

Resurrection and the Real Jesus

William Lane Craig

I am deeply indebted, not only to Dr. Crossan, but also to our four respondents for an extremely stimulating and wide-ranging exchange of ideas. I enjoyed enormously the debate itself, and I was fascinated by the different ways in which our commentators responded to it. Now I'd like to share my final reflections on the issues raised by the debate.

As the title of the debate indicates, the fundamental issue at stake is, Who is the real Jesus? By "real," one means something like "ultimately significant." Dr. Crossan and I chose this topic because we have radically divergent views of who the real Jesus is. I think that the real Jesus is the historical person who actually lived and wrought in first-century Palestine. For Dr. Crossan that historical individual is of marginal importance; the real Jesus is the Christ figure worshiped by the church. So in asking the real Jesus to please stand up, we were asking, Which of these two is the real Jesus? I especially liked the way the question was put because the act of standing up is analogous to Jesus' rising from the dead (in German, *auferstehen*), which I think provides the key to identifying the historical Jesus as the real Jesus.

Accordingly, in setting the groundwork for the debate in my opening speech, my aim was first to present a defense of my own answer to the question before us (Contention I: The real Jesus rose from the dead in confirmation of his radical personal claims to divinity) and then to offer a critique of Dr. Crossan's position on the issue (Contention II: If Contention I is false, Christianity is a fairy tale which no rational person should believe). Some of our commentators complained that important issues were left out of account or treated only superficially. But, believe me, no one is more acutely aware of this shortcoming in a debate situation than the debaters themselves. It's a daunting challenge to present in the space of twenty minutes—at a rate with which the audience can keep pace—not only a defense of one's own position with respect to Christ's person and work, but also an exposition and critique of the position of one's interlocutor. Vast issues must be summarized in a few terse sentences; words which our commentators freely employ, like "eschatological," "apocalyptic," and even "apologetics" would not be understood by a lay audience and so must be replaced by explanations of the concepts; citations from authorities must be whittled down to sound bites; the most important issues must alone be selected and condensed and secondary questions simply omitted. After the fat has been trimmed, one finds it necessary to begin cutting muscle and bone if the time constraints are to be observed. Important questions were therefore left aside. I can only beg the reader's indulgence and refer to my published work for a discussion of most of them.

That having been said, my final reflections will reexamine, in the light of our respondents' comments, the two basic contentions which I regard as central for a determination of an answer to the question, Who is the real Jesus?

Did the Real Jesus Rise from the Dead in Confirmation of His Radical Personal Claims to Divinity?

It is a remarkable feature of the debate that neither Dr. Crossan nor any of our respondents offered any refutation of the specific evidence in support of the contention that Jesus rose from the dead in confirmation of his personal claims to divinity. Certain caveats were added to some of my points, generalizations about the development of the Gospel traditions were enunciated, and some dissenting opinions were expressed, but there was almost no wrestling with the specific evidence I had adduced. Indeed, I must confess that certain comments of our respondents suggest that they regarded their critiques as an opportunity to express some of their pet peeves, since the positions they complain about are not at all the ones I formulated and defended. All this should become clear as we review my case for my first contention.

Jesus' Radical Personal Claims

Contention I includes two facts: first, that Jesus made radical personal claims to divinity; and, second, that he rose from the dead in confirmation of those claims. With respect to the first, I argued that Jesus "deliberately stood and spoke in the place of God himself." The phrase comes from the New Testament scholar Ernst Fuchs.[1] As is evident from my citation of Royce Gruenler in my closing remarks, I meant by this that "Jesus is consciously speaking as the voice of God on matters that belong only to God." He placed his own authority on a level with that of the divinely given law and even revised the law on his own authority, he claimed to rule the demonic powers of darkness, and he claimed to forgive sins. I certainly did not intend the ridiculous caricature drawn by Dr. Witherington which portrays Jesus as going about saying, "Hi, I'm God." Rather, I had in view precisely that "implicit Christology" mentioned by Dr. Blomberg and recognized by the mainstream of New Testament scholarship (in opposition to the attenuated portrait painted by the Jesus Seminar).[2] Contrary to Dr. Borg's view, Jesus' radical self-understanding is evident in the earliest layers of the tradition and among the demonstrably authentic sayings of Jesus, for example, the parable of the wicked tenants of the vineyard, the Sermon on the Mount, and his word on the time of his second coming. The context of Horst Georg Pöhlmann's remarks that were cited in my opening statement is worth quoting:

> This unheard-of claim to authority, as it comes to expression in the antitheses of the Sermon on the Mount, for example, is implicit Christology, since it presupposes a unity of Jesus with God that is deeper than that of all men, namely a unity of essence. This . . . claim to authority is explicable only from the side of his deity. This authority only God himself can claim.[3]

I am thus locating myself squarely in the mainstream of New Testament criticism with respect to Jesus' declarations about himself;

1. Norman Perrin, *A Modern Pilgrimage in New Testament Christology* (Philadelphia: Fortress, 1974), 52, states that Jesus "is acting, and implicitly claiming to act, as I once heard Ernst Fuchs express it in a class at the 'Kirchliche Hochschule' in Berlin, '*Als ob er an die Stelle Gottes stünde* [as if he stood in the very place of God himself].'"
2. For my defense of implicit Christology, see *Reasonable Faith* (Wheaton, Ill.: Crossway, 1994), ch. 7. For a critique of the Jesus portrayed by the Jesus Seminar, see *Jesus under Fire,* ed. Michael J. Wilkins and J. P. Moreland (Grand Rapids: Zondervan, 1995); and Luke Timothy Johnson, *The Real Jesus* (San Francisco: HarperCollins, 1996).
3. Horst Georg Pöhlmann, *Abriss der Dogmatik,* 3d rev. ed. (Düsseldorf: Patmos, 1966), 230.

I am not making the exaggerated claims rightly criticized by our respondents.

Dr. Witherington raises the very important question of "what sort of bridge can be built between Jesus' resurrection and claims about his divinity." I tried to deal with that issue in my opening speech in the citation from Wolfhart Pannenberg, where it is argued that the resurrection should be understood as "the divine vindication of the man who . . . [was] rejected as a blasphemer." I'm puzzled why Dr. Witherington goes on to attack the straw man position which states baldly that "the resurrection of Jesus proves his divinity." My position is exactly his own where he writes, "It is understandable and, in fact, biblical to argue that the resurrection shows that God vindicated Jesus and so vindicated his ministry and its implications. . . . The event itself was a sort of divine imprimatur on the life and ministry of Jesus."

This position seems to me eminently reasonable. A miracle without a context is inherently ambiguous. Its meaning can be found only in the religiohistorical context in which it occurred. So if God raised Jesus, who was executed because of his blasphemous claims, then the God who was supposedly blasphemed by Jesus has dramatically vindicated him and his claims. That means that Jesus really did have the authority to revise the Old Testament law, to rule over demons, and to forgive sins—that is to say, he was divine. I agree with Dr. Witherington that "the resurrection revealed what God really thought about Jesus, revealed who he truly was." And because the resurrection *revealed* who he truly was, it is not a private ontological claim, but an ontological claim that was manifested in history in a dramatic and unparalleled event and is therefore of evidential significance for who the real Jesus is.[4]

Jesus' Resurrection

INFERENCE TO THE RESURRECTION

The second point asserted by Contention I is that Jesus rose from the dead in confirmation of his claims. Notice the modesty and

---

4. It puzzles me that Dr. Witherington goes on to caution, "It is never adequate to assess just what was claimed about or even by Jesus historically. The question is, Are the claims true or not?" Of course! And that is why I do not argue from the radical claims taken in isolation, but from the resurrection in the context of and as the confirmation of those claims. The resurrection gives us good grounds for thinking those claims to be true.

the structure of my argument. Contrary to Dr. Miller's summation of my position, I do not assert that belief in the resurrection of Jesus "is the *only* reasonable option, and thus it would be irrational not to believe in it." Rather, I argue that four established facts (Jesus' burial, the empty tomb, postmortem appearances, and the origin of the Christian Way) "provide adequate inductive grounds for inferring Jesus' resurrection," and that "it's very difficult to deny that the resurrection of Jesus is the best explanation" of these four facts. Thus "there are good historical grounds for affirming that Jesus rose from the dead." In both my rebuttal and closing statement I reiterate that I see the resurrection as "the best explanation" of the relevant facts.

These statements are carefully chosen and indicate that I am employing inductive reasoning understood according to the model of inference to the best explanation.[5] This model holds that there may be a number of reasonable explanations for a body of evidence, and that one is to choose from this pool of live options that explanation which is the best, that is, which most successfully meets such criteria as having explanatory power, explanatory scope, and not being ad hoc. My claim is that the hypothesis "God raised Jesus from the dead" is the best explanation of the evidence discussed. I was prepared to argue this in the debate by comparing rival hypotheses in terms of the relevant criteria, but this inductive inference was not challenged in the debate, nor have any of the respondents challenged it. Again, I did not say that it is irrational to fail to believe in the resurrection, but rather that if Contention I is false, then it is irrational to believe in Christianity and in the resurrection in particular (Contention II).

The Factual Basis of the Inference

Contention I maintains that the resurrection of Jesus is the best explanation of four central facts. It will be helpful at this point to review those putative facts along with Dr. Crossan's position with respect to each (see figure 1).

But are the putative facts indeed facts? It would be the height of folly for me to go into a debate with one of the world's top New Testament critics and argue for the resurrection of Jesus on the basis of facts which are agreed to only, or even mostly, by conservative

---

5. See Peter Lipton, *Inference to the Best Explanation* (London: Routledge, 1991).

FIGURE 1

Putative Facts	Crossan's Position
1. After his crucifixion Jesus was buried by Joseph of Arimathea in his personal tomb.	1. Jesus' corpse was thrown into the common graveyard reserved for criminals and was probably eaten by dogs.
2. On the Sunday following the crucifixion, the tomb of Jesus was found empty by a group of his women followers.	2. The women's visit to the empty tomb was a fabrication made up by Mark.
3. On multiple occasions and under various circumstances different individuals and groups of people experienced appearances of Jesus alive from the dead.	3. The disciples never experienced any postmortem appearances of Jesus.
4. The original disciples believed that Jesus was risen from the dead despite their having every reason not to.	4. The disciples never really believed in the literal resurrection of Jesus at all.

scholars. As Dr. Miller suggests, that would hardly convince anybody! Therefore I was careful to base my case only on evidence which would be accepted by most New Testament scholars.[6] It may seem

6. Dr. Blomberg chides me for a "pattern of slight overstatement" concerning Facts (1) and (2). I accept the correction; but, quite honestly, it is amazing that the fundamental facts which inductively imply Jesus' resurrection are accepted by most New Testament scholars writing on these subjects. Take Fact (1). Dr. Blomberg refers to Raymond Brown's epochal commentary on the passion narratives as a demonstration of "the diversity of scholarly discussion" concerning the historicity of Joseph of Arimathea. This is hardly the case; Brown does not in fact cite any scholar as denying Joseph's historicity. What is denied by many scholars is Joseph's being a secret disciple or his conversation with Pilate, but these are no part of my Fact (1). Brown cites approvingly the verdict of Rudolf Bultmann, one of the twentieth century's most skeptical critics, on the burial account—"This is an historical account which creates no impression of being a legend, apart from the women . . . witnesses"—along with Vincent Taylor's judgment that Bultmann's verdict is "an understatement." Brown himself writes:

> I have been outlining a detectable pre-Gospel account of the burial of Jesus by Joseph. . . . How much of that is history? That Jesus was buried is historically certain. That Jewish sensitivity would have wanted this done before the oncoming Sabbath . . . is also certain, and our records give us no reason to think that this sensitivity was not honored. That the burial was done by Joseph of Arimathea is very probable, since a Christian fictional creation from nothing of a Jewish Sanhedrist who does what is right is almost

stupefying that while most New Testament critics who have written on these subjects accept the facts which, at least in my opinion, furnish inductive grounds for inferring the resurrection of Jesus, they do not themselves make that inference; but this is, in fact, the situation. It is Dr. Crossan's views on the four points which represent the minority position today. That is why, to Dr. Blomberg's consternation, Dr. Crossan honestly confesses to being on the side of the few. When Dr. Blomberg says that my position "is probably the minority view," that statement is accurate only if the position in question is the view

---

inexplicable, granted the hostility in early Christian writings toward the Jewish authorities responsible for the death of Jesus. . . . While high probability is not certitude, there is nothing in the basic pre-Gospel account of Jesus' burial by Joseph that could not plausibly be deemed historical. [Raymond E. Brown, *The Death of the Messiah*, 2 vols. (Garden City, N.Y.: Doubleday, 1994), 2:1240–41]

Strangely, Dr. Blomberg cites Kendall and O'Collins's article as "a recent example of scholarly skepticism," when in fact this article is a robust defense of Joseph's historicity over against Dr. Crossan's denial of it! They appeal to Bultmann, Fitzmyer, Porter, Gnilka, Hooker, "and many other biblical scholars who acknowledge an historically reliable core in the story of Joseph of Arimathea burying Jesus' body" (Daniel Kendall and Gerald O'Collins, "Did Joseph of Arimathea Exist?" *Biblica* 75 [1994]: 236). They acknowledge, nevertheless, that "every now and then the burial story is dismissed as completely non-historical" and cite Dr. Crossan as their sole example. But they note that "the standard recent commentators on Mark (Ernst, Gnilka, Haenchen, Harrington, Hooker, Pesch, Schweizer, etc.), . . . while recognizing the redactional contribution of the evangelist, do not invest him with the kind of creativity needed to invent the burial story as asserted by Crossan" (p. 240). In personal conversations at the Resurrection Summit (1996) and by phone, both O'Collins and Brown confirmed my judgment that only a decided minority of scholars who have written on the burial would deny the historicity of Joseph of Arimathea's entombment of Jesus.

As for Fact (2), Dr. Blomberg concurs with Jacob Kremer's verdict concerning scholarly acceptance of the biblical statements about the empty tomb (Kremer lists twenty-eight scholars; I can think of at least twenty more he neglected to mention). Blomberg questions, however, the consensus concerning the time and the women's role. But as these features of the narratives are unanimously present and supported as plausible by independent arguments, they are precisely among those features accepted by most exegetes. Note, too, that acceptance of the historicity of the empty tomb implies acceptance of the historicity of the burial of Jesus in a tomb rather than the common graveyard, and, since we have no story of Jesus' entombment other than the entombment by Joseph, scholars accepting Fact (2) naturally also accept Fact (1).

Dr. Blomberg thinks that Fact (3) is accurately stated, but "least significant." Here he is quite wrong; I would say that most scholars who argue for the historicity of Jesus' resurrection do so primarily on the fact of the appearances, appealing especially to Paul's list, and they then proceed to reject the hallucination hypothesis on grounds similar to those sketched by Dr. Witherington.

that Jesus rose historically from the dead. I freely grant that I may be in the minority there. But with respect to the four putative facts which serve as the inductive grounds for inferring to the resurrection, there I am comfortably in the mainstream.

I say all this, not because truth is determined by numbers, for it certainly is not; rather, it is precisely because, contrary to Dr. Miller's reading, I am interested in convincing outsiders that I appeal only to facts which would be accepted by the broad spectrum of scholarship, not just by conservatives. For that reason Dr. Miller is mistaken to portray the debate as a debate "about the historical accuracy of the resurrection stories in the Gospels." Nor is Dr. Borg correct in his assertion that I treat the Gospels "as straightforward historical documents" rather than "as a stream of developing tradition." I am basing my case on four broad facts established by the canons of biblical criticism, and this procedure is entirely compatible with the possibility of inconsistencies, inaccuracies, and fictional redactional additions in the Gospel resurrection narratives. We are not debating biblical inerrancy, but the historicity of the resurrection of Jesus. The latter does not imply the former. Pannenberg, for example, would agree with all four of the facts at issue and with the inference to the resurrection of Jesus despite his critical judgment that some of the appearance stories in the Gospels "have such a strongly legendary character that one can scarcely find a historical kernel of their own in them."[7] While my personal judgment may be more optimistic, nothing in my case depends on the adoption of a more conservative position.

In any case, what is important in the final analysis is not counting noses, but weighing the evidence, and I summarized several lines of evidence with respect to each of the four putative facts. Fully expecting these points to be vigorously disputed by Dr. Crossan, I came to the debate prepared to defend each of them; but Dr. Crossan, to my surprise, failed to contest a single piece of evidence which I adduced in support of the four main facts.

Dr. Miller seeks to undermine Facts (2) and (3) on the basis of "the many striking disparities [which] reinforce your doubts about the historical reliability of the stories." But a perusal of his comparative charts reveals that most of his disparities have been manufac-

---

7. Wolfhart Pannenberg, *Jesus—God and Man,* trans. Lewis L. Wilkins and Duane A. Priebe (Philadelphia: Westminster, 1968), 89.

tured. With respect to the Easter appearance stories, for example, a glance at the "Persons involved" column reveals that different appearances are being narrated; so it is wholly unwarranted to say that there is, for example, a disparity in the "Place" column because the women see Jesus between the tomb and the hideout whereas the Eleven and others see him appear in the upper room in Jerusalem. The sequence of the post-Easter appearance stories follows the logical pattern of Jerusalem-Galilee-Jerusalem, in line with the disciples' presence in Jerusalem for Passover and the Feast of Unleavened Bread, their return home to Galilee, and their visiting Jerusalem for Pentecost.[8] The empty-tomb accounts are more resistant to harmonization, though even they are remarkably consonant concerning such features as "Time," "Persons involved," "Position of the stone," and "Figures at the tomb."

More importantly, however, the sort of disparities in the secondary details pointed out by Dr. Miller do not suffice to undermine the historical core of the stories as stated in Facts (2) and (3). Remember: this is not a debate over biblical inerrancy. No professional historian jettisons his sources because disparities exist at points. To take an example from classical history, Livy and Polybius give us two irreconcilable accounts of Hannibal's crossing the Alps to attack Rome during the Second Punic War. But no historian doubts that Hannibal did carry out such a campaign.[9] When it comes to the empty-tomb narratives in the Gospels, Michael Grant, a professional historian, writes, "True, the discovery of the empty tomb is differently described by the various Gospels. . . . But if we apply the same sort of criteria that we would apply to any other ancient literary sources, then the evidence is firm and plausible enough to necessitate the conclusion that the tomb was indeed found empty."[10] As for the appearance narratives, the disparities to be found in records of the same event (e.g., Luke 24:36–43 and John 20:19–20) are trifling.

Dr. Miller also tries to cast doubts upon the historicity of the resurrection narratives by arguing that Matthew felt free to add to

8. See C. F. D. Moule, "The Post-Resurrection Appearances in Light of Festival Pilgrimages," *New Testament Studies* 4 (1957–58): 58–59.
9. I borrow the illustration from Murray J. Harris, *Raised Immortal* (Grand Rapids: Eerdmans, 1983), 68.
10. Michael Grant, *Jesus: An Historian's Review of the Gospels* (New York: Scribner, 1977), 176.

Mark's Gospel the story of the resurrection of the saints, a story which Matthew did not take literally, but saw as a figurative expression of the apocalyptic significance of Jesus' death. Dr. Miller's interpretation of this passage strikes me as quite persuasive, and probably only a few conservative scholars would treat the story as historical. But how does that conclusion cast doubt on the women's discovery of the empty tomb or the fact of the resurrection appearances?

The key premise in Dr. Miller's argument is his assertion, "since there is no good reason to regard Matthew 27:51–53 as an anomaly, we have to assume that it can help us understand Matthew's (and the other Evangelists') perspectives on the historical value of the stories in the Gospel." At this point, one has to grab for the reins and cry, "Whoa, Dr. Miller!" For this inference is obviously a rash overgeneralization predicated on a faulty foundation. In the first place, the antecedent of the premise is plausibly false, as Dr. Miller himself has demonstrated. For he has argued that the passage should not be taken literally precisely because of the apocalyptic language coloring the story. But the empty-tomb narrative is remarkable just for its simplicity and lack of apocalyptic embellishment. Wolfgang Nauck has observed that many theological motifs which one might have expected are conspicuously absent from the account, such as proof from prophecy, the in-breaking of the new eon, Jesus' descent into hell or the ascension of his spirit, the nature of the risen body, and the use of christological titles.[11] According to Kremer, theological reflection on the meaning of the resurrection is completely lacking, a fact which points to an early tradition.[12] Significantly, the Markan account lacks such elements as the earthquake and the resurrection of the saints so that we can see exactly where Matthew did and where he did not color his narrative with apocalyptic imagery. Thus we have good reason to see Matthew 27:51–53 as unusual in character. Since the antecedent of the key premise is false, Dr. Miller's argument is simply unsound.

More than that, however, even if the antecedent were true, the inductive base is far too slim to afford an inference as to Matthew's—

---

11. Wolfgang Nauck, "Die Bedeutung des leeren Grabes für den Glauben an den Auferstandenen," *Zeitschrift für die neutestamentliche Wissenschaft* 47 (1956): 243–67.

12. Jacob Kremer, "Zur Diskussion über 'das leere Grab,'" in *Resurrexit*, ed. Edouard Dhanis (Rome: Libreria Editrice Vaticana, 1974), 153.

much less the other Evangelists'!—perspectives on the historical value of the Gospel stories in general. That this inference is overdrawn is obvious from the fact that it would prove too much: it would justify historical skepticism concerning everything in the Gospels, which is absurd. With respect to Jesus' passion, Luke Johnson, a New Testament scholar at Emory University, observes, "The support for the mode of his death, its agents, and perhaps its coagents, is overwhelming: Jesus faced a trial before his death, was condemned, and was executed by crucifixion."[13] No New Testament scholar would think that the historicity of Jesus' crucifixion is called into question because of Matthew's use of apocalyptic imagery in describing his death. Thus Dr. Miller's inductive base is simply inadequate to support so sweeping a generalization as that Matthew was indifferent to the historicity of the stories in the Gospel. The inference is even more evidently fallacious when it is extended by extrapolation to the other Evangelists as well.

Dr. Miller does try to provide some independent justification for historical skepticism concerning the Gospel narratives on the basis of the Evangelists' freedom in reshaping the traditions they received. He mentions specifically Matthew's alterations of Mark's empty-tomb story. But how does Dr. Miller know that Matthew's differences here are due to Matthean editorial activity? That Matthew was dependent upon prior tradition rather than writing creatively is clear from his account of the guards.[14] Thus it is plausible that in the empty-tomb story Matthew is drawing upon non-Markan tradition as well as Mark. It is not a matter, then, of Matthew's treating Mark with historical indifference, but of Matthew's trying to integrate his sources. In any case, Dr. Miller really exaggerates the disparities between Mark and Matthew. What the stories actually show is how faithful Matthew remains to the basic Markan account. Once one realizes that the story of the guards represents an independent tradition which Matthew has integrated with the Markan account of the women's discovery of the empty tomb, the differences are negligible.[15]

13. Johnson, *Real Jesus,* 125.

14. Matthew 28:15 makes it evident that there is a tradition history behind the story, as do both the many words in the narrative which appear uniquely here in the New Testament and some non-Matthean stylistic traits.

15. E.g., Mark's "young man" is intended to be an angelic figure, as is evident from his white robe and the women's reaction of fear, and is so understood by the other Evangelists.

Dr. Miller's argument at best proves that Matthew did not regard Mark's account or his own account as "a literal report of an actual event." The emphasis here lies on the word *literal,* understood in the sense of "inerrant in every detail." But this conclusion is compatible with the view that the empty-tomb story is a fundamentally or generally reliable report of an actual event. That is more than is required for the establishment of Fact (2). Dr. Miller allows that there may be in the empty-tomb story "a historical kernel" which is "literally true," but he thinks that we have no way of telling. But, I ask, how can he make that judgment as long as he is content to remain with generalities and does not engage the specific evidence for the empty tomb (and appearances), crucial components of which are not even based on the Gospels?

Dr. Borg reiterates the view that the resurrection and the narratives of it are metaphorical in character. But he fails to interact with the several points put forward in my rebuttal to show that the early Christians took the resurrection to be a literal event (see also Dr. Witherington's comments). Nor does he respond to what I consider the powerful argument that the early Christians had in the doctrine of the Holy Spirit a theologically rich way of expressing Christ's continuing presence without resorting to misleading metaphorical talk of resurrection from the dead.

The bottom line is that not a single point of the evidence which I brought forth in support of the four central facts undergirding the inference to the resurrection of Jesus was challenged by either Dr. Crossan or any of our four respondents. Thus we have good reason to accept these four facts, as most New Testament scholars have.

DR. CROSSAN'S POSITION

Consider now Dr. Crossan's four counterpoints to the four central facts undergirding the resurrection. Here I argued that Dr. Crossan's conclusions were based on several idiosyncratic and implausible presuppositions, such that no confidence can be reposed in those conclusions. Again, I came to the debate fully expecting a lively exchange concerning these presuppositions, but my preparation proved superfluous, as Dr. Crossan made almost no effort to defend his presuppositions.

Dr. Borg thinks that Dr. Crossan's failure to respond is of little significance, since it would make no difference if he were wrong about the first two presuppositions, namely, the priority of the account in the Gospel of Peter and the Secret Gospel of Mark. But I think Dr. Borg does not appreciate how crucial these presuppositions are to Dr. Crossan's case. He needs the priority of the Gospel of Peter to deprive the canonical Gospels of any historical worth with respect to Jesus' fate. By making the account in the Gospel of Peter the only source of the canonical burial and resurrection narratives, Dr. Crossan is able to dismiss the canonical narratives as making no historical contribution at all to our understanding of Jesus' fate. Moreover, by means of his methodological principle of ignoring material not multiply attested even if it is found in the earliest stratum of tradition, Dr. Crossan can safely ignore even the Gospel of Peter's testimony to the resurrection. But deny the priority of the account in the Gospel of Peter, and all of a sudden one has to deal with the question of the historicity of the canonical burial, empty tomb, and appearance traditions.

Similarly, Dr. Crossan's appeal to the Secret Gospel of Mark is crucial for how he deals with the women witnesses to the empty tomb, a feature of Mark's narrative so strongly emphasized by Dr. Witherington. Dr. Crossan sees the women as residue left over from the objectionable passages in the Secret Gospel of Mark. But deny the hypothesis of a prior Secret Gospel of Mark, and the force of Dr. Witherington's argument for the historicity of the women's discovering the tomb empty becomes very powerful.

Now what the lay reader needs to understand is how positively bizarre these first two presuppositions are. According to Thomas Wright, the primacy of the Gospel of Peter account "has not been accepted yet by any other serious scholar."[16] The Secret Gospel of Mark hypothesis has only a tiny minority of scholars in its camp

16. N. T. Wright, *Jesus and the Victory of God* (Minneapolis: Fortress, 1996), 49. Recalling Raymond Brown's 1986 presidential address to the Society of New Testament Studies, which exposed the weakness in Dr. Crossan's hypothesis of the priority of the Gospel of Peter, Kendall and O'Collins, "Joseph of Arimathea," 237–38, note that while "one might have expected Crossan to have explicitly answered this very public challenge," he failed to do so in any of his subsequent books. Moreover,

apart from one or two sympathetic reactions, scholars generally have remained quite unconvinced by Crossan's 1988 lengthy and tortuous attempt to rehabilitate the *Gospel of Peter* and claim that its core . . . served as the sole source for Mark's story of the passion (and resurrection). The reviews . . . by Black, Fuller, Green, Matera, Meier and Wink . . . were little less than devastating in demolishing Crossan's case for an early date for the core of the *Gospel of Peter* and literary dependence from it on the part of Mark and other canonical gospels.

and has received devastating criticism. Thus, despite what Dr. Blomberg characterizes as "a considerable scattering of unpublished or little-known university professors" who have bought into the views of the Jesus Seminar, my point remains that no major New Testament scholar accepts all of Dr. Crossan's four presuppositions.[17] Again, I say this merely to emphasize that Dr. Crossan's rejection of the four facts supporting the resurrection hypothesis is predicated upon extremely controversial assumptions which beg some justification—justification which, at least in this exchange, has not been forthcoming.

Now Dr. Crossan does make some response concerning his fourth presupposition, which I characterized as naturalism, the view that "miracles are impossible." He at first emphatically declares that he absolutely rejects naturalism. But then in his rebuttal he takes back with the left hand what the right has given: "The supernatural *always* (at least till this is disproved for me) operates through the screen of the natural."[18] But that *is* naturalism. Naturalism holds that every event in the space-time order has a cause which is also part of the space-time order. There are no events which are the immediate products of supernatural causes. Naturalists need not be atheists. The deists, for example, were theistic naturalists: God acts in the world only mediately through natural causes. Now this is exactly Dr. Crossan's position. Consider his discussion of inexplicable events in the dialogue portion of the debate. Someone else might say, "I believe God has intervened here"; but Dr. Crossan states, "It's a theological presupposition of mine that God does not operate that way." That is precisely an affirmation of the fourth presupposition which I identified.

Now what is the significance of this theological presupposition for the historical Jesus? Very simply, it rules out in advance the historicity of events like the resurrection since there are no natural causes which could plausibly serve as the "screen" or intermediate

17. Dr. Blomberg's citation of Robert W. Funk with Mahlon H. Smith, *The Gospel of Mark: Red-letter Edition* (Sonoma, Calif.: Polebridge, 1991), does not in fact support his claim that the Jesus Seminar has accepted all four of Dr. Crossan's presuppositions, for Funk and Smith say not a word about the Gospel of Peter as a literary source of the Gospels, though they do accept Secret Mark. In fact, the spring 1996 meeting of the Jesus Seminar voted against Crossan's view on the priority of the account in the Gospel of Peter.

18. Dr. Blomberg has, unfortunately, not seen Dr. Crossan's argument for what it really is.

cause whereby God effects such an event. The resurrection so transcends the powers of natural agents in the world that it would require an immediate act of God—in other words, a miracle—in order to occur, and this Dr. Crossan rules out a priori. Thus his antisupernaturalism determines his skepticism concerning the historicity of the New Testament witness to the resurrection of Jesus.

The question which now becomes unavoidable is, What justification is there for the presupposition of naturalism?[19] Unfortunately, despite the ubiquity of this presupposition among skeptical critics, it is one which New Testament scholars are ill equipped to discuss. For this presupposition is philosophical in nature, and most New Testament scholars are poorly trained in this field. Fortunately, Christian philosophers have written extensively on this subject, and I know of no good reason to adopt the presupposition of naturalism.[20] Short of a proof of atheism, one has to be open to the possibility that God has acted immediately in the world and thus also to evidence that he has.

As I review the response to my first major contention, what is striking is the almost complete absence of any refutation of the evidence for the historicity of the resurrection of Jesus. Its detractors speak only in generalities and do not grapple with specific points. Until they descend from the realm of generalization and engage

19. Dr. Borg does offer two objections to the idea of God's unmediated action in the world: (1) it is inexplicable why God does not intervene more often; and (2) this notion privileges Christianity, and thus is inconsistent with God's grace. But (1) is really the question of theodicy, which is hardly solved by saying that God never intervenes. One could ask Dr. Borg, Why does God never intervene to stop suffering? Is he unable or unwilling? We all know how the argument proceeds from there. (On the problem of evil, see Alvin Plantinga, *God, Freedom, and Evil* [New York: Harper and Row, 1974].) As for (2), this is really the problem of Christian exclusivism, which is hardly solved by denying God's immediate action in the world. An exclusivistic nonsupernatural Christianity still faces Borg's problem, and a supernaturalistic Christianity does not automatically restrict all miracles to Christian miracles. In any case, there are other solutions to how Christianity can be objectively true and yet God's grace universally accessible (see, e.g., William Lane Craig, "'No Other Name': A Middle Knowledge Perspective on the Exclusivity of Salvation through Christ," *Faith and Philosophy* 6 [1989]: 172–88).

20. The best published treatment is still Richard Swinburne, *The Concept of Miracle* (New York: Macmillan, 1970). A recent short treatment is Steve Clark, "When to Believe in Miracles," *American Philosophical Quarterly* 34 (1997): 95–102. A popular anthology is *In Defense of Miracles,* ed. R. Douglas Geivett and Gary R. Habermas (Downers Grove, Ill.: InterVarsity, 1997).

themselves with the specific evidence adduced, their skepticism concerning the historicity of the resurrection of Jesus, and hence concerning the identification of the historical Jesus as the real Jesus, remains unjustified.

If Jesus Did Not Rise, Is Christianity a Fairy Tale Which No Rational Person Should Believe?

In my second contention, I turned to offer a critique of Dr. Crossan's alternative view of the real Jesus. It's extremely important to understand what that view is, if we are to appreciate the force of my critique. Dr. Blomberg could not be more mistaken when he portrays the difference between Crossan and me as the difference between evidentialism and fideism. As I have made clear elsewhere,[21] I am not an evidentialist, if by that term is meant someone who holds that Christian faith is based on evidence. I see faith in Christ as what epistemologists call a properly basic belief which is grounded in the witness of God's Holy Spirit. Thus, I am not contending that belief in Christianity is irrational in the absence of evidence. Rather, I am claiming that belief in Christianity is irrational if Jesus of Nazareth did not rise from the dead. More specifically, it is irrational to believe in Christ if Jesus was just a mortal human who died and rotted away.

Dr. Crossan's view involves a sharp bifurcation between the Jesus of history and the Christ of faith. The former is the purely human figure from Nazareth; the latter is the divine person worshiped by the church. It is the latter, in Dr. Crossan's view, who is the real Jesus. It is not that this divine figure really exists; this figure is real only in the sense of being of ultimate significance. Dr. Crossan associates Jesus with the realm of facts and Christ with the realm of interpretation. Thus, in the name Jesus Christ, "the first word, *Jesus,* is a *fact* open in principle to proof and disproof (he did or did not exist). The second word, *Christ* (or Lord, or Wisdom, or Son of God, etc.), is an *interpretation,* not open in principle to proof or disproof (he is or is not such)."[22] The Christ of faith is thus not a factual reality, but an interpretation which a believer puts on Jesus of Nazareth. "To say that Jesus is divine . . . means for me that *I* see *Jesus* as the manifestation of *God.*"[23]

21. Craig, *Reasonable Faith*, ch. 1.
22. John Dominic Crossan, *Who Killed Jesus?* (San Francisco: Harper, 1995), 217.
23. Ibid., 215–16.

The difference between Dr. Crossan's view and mine is thus the difference between objectivism and nonobjectivism, between realism and antirealism. Dr. Crossan is an antirealist about such theological statements as "Christ died for our sins," "Christ rose from the dead," "Christ loves all people," and so on. These are not factual statements at all, but just interpretive statements, ways of seeing the world.

Using the playful illustration of Peter Pan (remember, this was a debate before a live audience!), I presented what I take to be a crushing critique of Dr. Crossan's position.[24] If the historical Jesus is not factually divine, then to worship Jesus Christ as divine is either to worship a dead man—which is idolatry—or to worship a figment of our imagination—which is self-delusion. I can't see any way out of this dilemma, and neither Dr. Crossan nor any of our respondents has suggested one.[25]

24. This critique is an old and familiar one. John A. T. Robinson, *The Human Face of God* (Philadelphia: Westminster, 1973), 126, for example, warned: "Immunity from the critics has been bought at the price of cutting the dependence of the Christ of faith on the Jesus of history (except for his bare existence and death on the cross). The result has been a dangerous dichotomy which is in peril not merely of producing a split mind in the critical believer, but of reintroducing a docetic Christ-figure impervious to history because untouched by it."

25. Dr. Borg's attempt to argue that Jesus' fate is irrelevant to the truth of Easter is itself based on irrelevancies. (1) Of course there is a distinction between resuscitation and resurrection, as he says; but no one thinks Jesus was merely resuscitated, and it is not explained how a man could be risen if (contrary to Jewish conception) his corpse remained in the tomb. (2) Paul's doctrine of the nature of the resurrection body is irrelevant to the divorce between Jesus' corpse and the risen Christ, since in Paul's conception the resurrection involves a transformation of, and hence numerical identity with, the body that is interred. (3) Taking the resurrection narratives metaphorically is a question-begging defense since the very question is the legitimacy of construing them that way.

Allow me to say something further concerning (2). Dr. Borg gives two reasons for construing Jesus' resurrection as nonphysical: (a) Paul regards his own visionary experience as typical, and (b) a spiritual body is nonphysical. Concerning (a) I agree with Dr. Crossan that Paul does not treat the resurrection appearances to the disciples as being of the same nature as his Damascus road experience: "Paul needs, in 1 Corinthians 15:1–11, to equate his own experience with that of the preceding apostles. To equate, that is, its validity and legitimacy but not necessarily its mode or manner. Jesus *was revealed* to all of them, but Paul's own entranced revelation should not be presumed to be the model for all others" (John Dominic Crossan, *Jesus: A Revolutionary Biography* [San Francisco: Harper, 1994], 169).

Concerning (b), will Dr. Borg pretend that as the opposite of the natural man, the spiritual man is nonphysical and immaterial? Will he deny that for Paul an immaterial,

In my rebuttal, I pushed this critique another notch forward. By making a rigid dichotomy between the Jesus of history and the Christ of faith, Dr. Crossan has lost all constraints on who the Christ of faith is. In addition to Jonestown and Waco, we now have the tragedy of the Heaven's Gate suicides to underline the importance of assessing the objective, factual truth of our religious beliefs. Quoting Dr. Crossan himself, I asked why we should accept the Christ myth rather than any other, since none is objectively true; and no answer from Dr. Crossan or our respondents has been forthcoming.

The turning point in the debate came, in my opinion, during the dialogue portion, when I pressed Dr. Crossan on whether the theological statement "God exists" is a statement of fact or a statement of faith (an interpretation). Reread that section closely. In affirming that "God exists" is a statement of faith, Dr. Crossan implies that this is just an interpretation which a believer puts on reality; from a factual point of view, God does not exist. Dr. Crossan struggles valiantly to elude this implication by stating that it is meaningless to ask how God would be if no human beings existed. But this question is grammatically well formed and clearly meaningful, as is his question, "Would I be annoyed if I hadn't been conceived?" (That is what my kids call a "no-duh" question; obviously if you hadn't been conceived, you wouldn't be annoyed, since you wouldn't exist!)

So did God exist during the Jurassic age? Was there a Creator and Sustainer of the universe at that time? Dr. Crossan finally comes

---

unextended body is a contradiction in terms? If it is not, then what is the distinction between the resurrection of the body and the immortality of the soul? The answer to Dr. Crossan's question about Jesus' preresurrection body is straightforward: yes, Jesus had a *sōma psychikon,* a natural body, during his earthly existence. Though Jesus was fully yielded to the Spirit, he nevertheless possessed a body which bore the traits of our fallen humanity, viz., mortality and corruptibility. Thus Paul can boldly say that he "who knew no sin" (2 Cor. 5:21) came "in the likeness of sinful flesh, and to deal with sin" (Rom. 8:3 NRSV). Paul does not mean that the flesh in the sense of the physical body is itself sinful or evil, but that it bears the lingering effects of sin. Thus Jesus fully identified with our fallen state in taking a mortal body, yet without committing sin himself.

Dr. Borg queries how the historical Jesus can live in my heart today. What I mean is that the exalted Christ whom I love and worship and who is at work in my life today is the same person as (i.e., is numerically identical with) the person who lived in first-century Palestine. These are not two different persons, as they are for Dr. Borg. The New Testament does not inform us about the state of the ascended Christ's body, but we know that when the risen Lord is present in our three-dimensional universe, then his body becomes evident and locatable.

clean and says he'd prefer to say no. Now if God does not exist independently of the human imagination, if God is just a projection of human consciousness, if it is we who create God rather than God who creates us, then how is this any different from what my atheist friends believe? What this exchange revealed is that on a factual level Dr. Crossan's view is, as I suspected, atheism. "God" is just an interpretive construct which human beings put on the universe in the same way that "Christ" is an interpretive construct which Christian believers put on the purely human Jesus. In this light, it is no surprise at all that Dr. Crossan believes neither in miracles nor in the resurrection of Jesus as events of history. For, from a factual perspective, there really is no such person or being as God to bring about these events.

John Dominic Crossan is thus a good example of contemporary theologians who have accepted the modernist critique of religion but who cannot bring themselves, in Don Cupitt's phrase, to "take leave of God."[26] I agree with Cupitt that once that critique has been embraced, God should be dispensed with. It is just irrational to worship someone who really isn't there. But, of course, the better alternative is to challenge the modernist critique and to affirm classical Christian theism. As I have tried to show in Contention I, when we take that step we are moving in line with, and not against, the evidence.

Concluding Remarks

We have seen good grounds for thinking that the historical Jesus, not the mythical Jesus propounded by Dr. Crossan, is the real Jesus. But so what? Is Dr. Miller correct that "very, very few, if any at all," outsiders will be persuaded by such arguments? Is it true that "almost no Hindus, Buddhists, Jews, or Muslims (to name only some), nor atheists or agnostics will be persuaded" by arguments like these? Am I really just preaching to the choir?

Now a careful reading of Dr. Miller's fascinating remarks on the efficacy of Christian apologetics reveals that his conclusion is not that these arguments are unsound or inherently implausible or not worth putting forth to unbelievers. Rather, his point is the curious conclusion that since apologetics is intended for insiders, therefore the Gospels likewise are intended for insiders (and so need not be taken literally).

26. Don Cupitt, *Taking Leave of God* (New York: Crossroad, 1981).

Now it may remain a moot issue whether the Gospels intend to convince outsiders. The Gospels of both Luke and John do have a heavy emphasis on the notion of witness, as Allison Trites has shown. He points out that Luke-Acts presents the claims of Christ against a background of hostility, contention, and active persecution, which accounts for the large place given to juridical terminology and ideas drawn from the law court. According to Trites, the operative question for Luke is, On what grounds or evidence can people have faith? Hence he put the greatest possible emphasis on the factual content of preaching. Similarly, in John the concept of witness is apologetic and juridical.[27] His avowed purpose is to convince people that Jesus is the Christ (John 20:31).[28]

But never mind. The question I would rather raise is, Is apologetics really intended for insiders? Are these arguments really so ineffectual with outsiders? And if so, why bother to engage in presenting them to outsiders?

Now a large part of Dr. Miller's case that Christian apologetics is intended for insiders is based on the fact that the debate with Dr. Crossan was held at Moody Church and published by Baker Book House. It was intriguing to see what a different take Dr. Blomberg had on this fact. And I must say that Dr. Blomberg is closer to the truth here. Turner-Welninski & Associates, which hosted and taped the debate, wanted the event held in the inner city of Chicago, and, after checking several possible venues, including Dr. Crossan's DePaul University (capacity too small) and the Blackstone Theater (price too high), finally settled on Moody Church because of its large auditorium, affordability, and just the ease of working with fellow evangelicals in pulling off such an event. Tickets were distributed through Catholic bookstores in the city, and evangelicals were encouraged to bring along their non-Christian friends. (Actually, I very rarely lecture or debate in a church; usually such events take place on university campuses before audiences that are predominantly composed of outsiders.) As for the selection of Baker, it is extraordinarily difficult to interest nonevangelical presses in publishing a defense of the historical resurrection of

27. Allison A. Trites, *The New Testament Concept of Witness* (New York: Cambridge University Press, 1977), 78–90.
28. See D. A. Carson, "The Purpose of the Fourth Gospel: John 20:31 Reconsidered," *Journal of Biblical Literature* 106 (1987): 639–51.

Jesus.[29] Thus, Dr. Miller is simply in error when he asserts that the site and publisher of the debate are indications that the intended audience of arguments for the historicity of the resurrection is insiders.

Notice, furthermore, that Dr. Miller's skepticism about the efficacy of arguments for Jesus' burial, empty tomb, appearances, and the origin of the Christian Way does not prevent him from presenting historical arguments for his own conclusions. In arguing for the nonhistorical character of Matthew 27:51–53, he uses expressions like "it is inconceivable" that no other source should mention the event, "historians have no real choice but to conclude that the events in Matthew 27:51–53 did not really happen," and "historians are not free to claim that something happened simply because they want it to be so—just as juries are not free to reach any verdict they want. Historians and juries must be guided by evidence." Now this is very confusing. Dr. Miller seems to treat his own historical arguments as probative and assumption-free, but the historical arguments for the credibility of the Gospel narratives as assumption-laden and nugatory. He cannot have it both ways, since the same historical method is being used in both cases. Dr. Miller has either to admit that his own arguments are really only for those inside his camp or to allow that historical arguments for the resurrection might, like his own arguments, be intended for outsiders.

Now if Christian apologetics is intended for outsiders as well as insiders, is it as ineffectual as Dr. Miller claims? Here I agree with him that only a few outsiders will be convinced by such arguments, and I have said as much.[30] Now why is this? Dr. Miller says that the "big reason" that "informed, intelligent, sincere, and spiritual people are almost never persuaded by apologetics" is that "most apologists use assumptions that only insiders take for granted." I suspect that this answer is far too intellectualist, that all sorts of emotional, social, and moral factors also conspire to block the efficacy of an argument; but let that pass for now. What I don't understand is how Dr. Miller's answer differs from my own point that the reason Dr. Crossan rejects the evidence for the resurrection is his presuppositions. I said that in inferring to the best explanation one chooses from a pool of live options the explanation that best fulfils

29. I could tell some personal anecdotes here, but I shall leave that aside.
30. Craig, *Reasonable Faith*, 50.

certain criteria. But if some explanation is not even in the pool of live options, it will not be taken seriously. For example, someone who presupposes naturalism won't even consider the hypothesis "God raised Jesus from the dead" to be a candidate for the best explanation. The British New Testament scholar R. T. France has written:

> At the level of their literary and historical character we have good reason to treat the gospels seriously as a source of information on the life and teaching of Jesus, and thus on the historical origins of Christianity. . . . Indeed many ancient historians would count themselves fortunate to have four such responsible accounts, written within a generation or two of the events, and preserved in such a wealth of manuscript evidence. . . . Beyond that point, the decision as to how far a scholar is willing to accept the record they offer is likely to be influenced more by his openness to a "supernaturalist" world-view than by strictly historical considerations.[31]

Now if someone is not open to supernaturalism, do we just throw up our hands in despair and terminate the discussion? I don't see that this is necessary. Rather than giving up, what we then need to do is to explore his presuppositions and assumptions. Discussion need not abruptly end; insiders and outsiders can discuss the rational justification (or lack thereof) for their respective assumptions. Thus I don't see that Dr. Miller has provided a reason for abandoning the apologetic enterprise toward outsiders (nor did he claim to have done so); rather, we are called to a deeper level of inquiry and argument.

Finally, I am by no means so pessimistic as Dr. Miller about the efficacy of apologetic argumentation vis-à-vis outsiders. Even if few people are directly convinced by our arguments to become Christians, still we should not underestimate the leavening power of rational defenses of the Christian faith to foster an intellectual milieu in which Christian belief is a live option for unbelievers. In 1913 J. Gresham Machen warned:

> False ideas are the greatest obstacles to the reception of the gospel. We may preach with all the fervor of a reformer and yet succeed only in winning a straggler here and there, if we permit the whole collective thought of the nation or of the world to be controlled by ideas which,

31. R. T. France, "The Gospels as Historical Sources for Jesus, the Founder of Christianity," *Truth* 1 (1985): 86.

by the resistless force of logic, prevent Christianity from being re-garded as anything more than a harmless delusion.[32]

The situation feared by Machen already exists in Europe. Having lived in Europe for over thirteen years, I can testify that evangelism is immeasurably more difficult in that context than in North America because the prevailing European culture is so deeply post-Christian. In our country, the Jesus Seminar and its parent organization the Wes-tar Institute are, as Johnson points out, engaged primarily in "carry-ing out a cultural mission" to reshape how our society sees Jesus.[33] For the evangelical church to remain silent at such a time as this and to allow the caricature of Jesus propounded by the Jesus Seminar to go uncontested would be an ill-conceived strategy indeed. Even if few people become Christians as a direct result of an apologetic argument, such defenses do help to shape and preserve an intellectual milieu in which faith in the Jesus of the New Testament is still a rational alter-native for most persons in our culture.

And even in individual cases, it has not been my experience that so desperately few find apologetic arguments persuasive. I once gave a lecture at the University of Alberta in Edmonton on "Five Reasons Why God Exists and Three Reasons It Makes a Difference." My five reasons included the cosmological, teleological, and moral argu-ments, the evidence for Jesus' resurrection, and personal experience. Several students during the question-and-answer time were quite hostile. It seemed that I had persuaded no one. But a letter I later re-ceived from Gabriel Ting, a staff member with Campus Crusade for Christ at the university, informed me that six people had decided to become Christians as a result of the talk.

Again, I think of a couple of debates in which I participated at the University of Illinois. Mark Ashton, the local InterVarsity director, tells me that twenty students committed their lives to Christ at that time and that as many as forty more have joined investigative Bible studies geared to helping unbelievers learn more about Jesus Christ. We can praise God for his work of grace in the life of each student.

I recently visited Willow Creek Community Church in the Chi-cago area, where I met John Swift, a successful investment banker who was being baptized that Sunday. He told a remarkable story, a

32. J. Gresham Machen, "Christianity and Culture," *Princeton Theological Re-view* 11 (1913): 7.
33. Johnson, *Real Jesus,* 6.

copy of which was given to me. As an unbeliever he had felt spiritually bankrupt: "I wanted to believe in Jesus, but I could not bring myself to accept the supernaturalness of His resurrection. . . . I had spent a life as a professional skeptic and belief in the supernatural did not come easy." He joined a small group at the church and talked with one of the ministers, Mark Mittelberg, who laid out for him the evidence for Jesus' miraculous resurrection. John's testimony continues:

> Mark listened to my questions and suggested some references I might want to look at and, in fact, lent me the book that made the difference. The book was *Jesus under Fire*, specifically the chapter . . . refuting the Jesus Seminar's version of the Resurrection. After reading the entire book and that chapter twice, on March 17, 1996, I realized my questions had been answered, and I asked Jesus into my life. It still gives me goosebumps.

This is a beautiful example of how Christian apologetics should work: a person with a searching heart troubled by certain questions; a loving community; intelligent answers.

Of course, the detractor of apologetics might say that people like John are few, and I suppose he would be right. But one of those few might turn out to be a C. S. Lewis,[34] who will go on to influence countless others for Christ. And even if none of them does, should that matter? Didn't Jesus say that the shepherd will leave the ninety-and-nine and go to find the one lost sheep? Isn't one John Swift worth the effort? Here it is I who am on the side of the few.

---

34. In his *Surprised by Joy* (New York: Harcourt, Brace, 1955), 223–24, Lewis recounts the pivotal event in his becoming a Christian:

> Early in 1926 the hardest boiled of all the atheists I ever knew sat in my room on the other side of the fire and remarked that the evidence for the historicity of the Gospels was really surprisingly good. "Rum thing," he went on. "All that stuff of Frazer's about the Dying God. Rum thing. It almost looks as if it had really happened once." To understand the shattering impact of it, you would need to know the man (who has certainly never since shown any interest in Christianity). If he, the cynic of cynics, the toughest of the toughs, were not—as I would still have put it—"safe," where could I turn? Was there then no escape?

Lewis later yielded his life to his divine Pursuer.

Index

Paul Copan is a Ph.D. candidate at Marquette University. Formerly an adjunct professor at Trinity International University, he is currently on staff with Ravi Zacharias International Ministries in Norcross, Georgia. He lives with his wife Jacqueline and their five children in Suwanee, Georgia. He is the author of *"True for You, but Not for Me."*